Praise for
The Truth About Negotiations

"Armed with cutting-edge research, Thompson offers up the definitive answers that propel even seasoned negotiators to reach the next level of negotiation success. Each chapter provides a clear answer to a burning question, and the return-on-investment is monumental."

— **Tanios Viviani**, President-Americas, Amway Corp.

"Conflict and adversarial situations are unavoidable, particularly in the security industry. Thompson's lessons, however, offer a roadmap to navigating those interactions successfully. I found myself using her lessons the same day I learned from her, turning potential conflict into a win/win for all parties involved. You need these tools in your toolbox!"

— **Ben Keller**, CPP, Senior Director, Corporate Security Services, Capital One

"Being successful in today's highly competitive business environment requires being committed to helping customers reach their goals as much as we're trying to reach our own. This very insightful and powerful book makes clear that a consultative approach is fundamental to a successful negotiation. It shows how we can actually expand the pie—with both sides receiving more than expected—if we take the time to really understand the interests of the other."

— **Tony Likovich**, Vice President, Business Development, Truven Health Analytics

THE TRUTH ABOUT

NEGOTIATIONS

Leigh Thompson

Library of Congress Control Number: 2013936133

Fourth Printing: February 2015

Vice President, Publisher
Tim Moore

Associate Publisher and Director of Marketing
Amy Neidlinger

Acquisitions Editor
Jeanne Levine

Operations Specialist
Jodi Kemper

Marketing Manager
Megan Graue

Cover and Interior Designs
Stuart Jackman,
Dorling Kindersley

Design Manager
Sandra Schroeder

Managing Editor
Kristy Hart

Senior Project Editor
Jovana Shirley

Copy Editor
Kitty Wilson

Proofreader
Julie Anderson

Senior Compositor
Gloria Schurick

Manufacturing Buyer
Dan Uhrig

Introduction

You spend more time negotiating than you do driving to work each day. Most of us take our driving seriously: We've studied, practiced, and taken a driving test. We have a license, insurance, a car, and a fancy navigation system; we know the rules of the road, and we hope that people who disobey those rules will get pulled over and ticketed. These investments mean that we don't sit up at night worrying about how we are going to drive ourselves to work. We have the equipment, we know what we are doing, and we get there. We feel ready, prepared.

Negotiating every day should be the same way. Yet, if you are like most other people, you spend countless hours fretting about upcoming negotiations. "What should I say?" "Should I open first or not?" "What do I do if they don't accept my offer?" and so on.

This book is about how to make sure you are prepared and ready to negotiate on the roughest of terrain, with the most daunting road conditions.

The need to negotiate can happen at any time—sometimes once a day, and sometimes more than once a day. Any time you cannot reach your goals without the cooperation of someone else, you are propelled headlong into negotiation. You may not be engaged in a hostage negotiation, or striking a deal for millions of dollars' worth of a product or service for a company, but the importance of arriving at a point where you and the other party both feel you win is vital to your peace, sanity, and productivity. For example, if your goal is to eat dinner in peace, and your young child is demanding that you fix a toy or play a game, you must negotiate.

If your goal is to sell your house and upgrade to a nicer house with a heftier mortgage, you must negotiate with your penny-pinching spouse, who may not be up for the move. You sometimes are thrown into negotiations when you least expect it—such as when somebody has the nerve to claim what you thought was yours. Imagine that a coworker announces he or she wants to "reconsider" the project responsibilities that you thought you both already agreed to. Or say that your neighbor claims it is your job to repair a fence that fell down after a freak thunderstorm.

The simple question I ask in this book is "Are you ready to negotiate at the drop of a hat?" If your answer is anything but "Yes, certainly," then please read on. One false move in negotiations of major importance, such as salary negotiations, house buying, and car buying, can have a dramatic negative consequence on your economic welfare for years to come. Given that your quality of life is affected by your ability to bring home the bacon as well as eat it in quiet dignity, knowing how to negotiate in the corporate world and in the kitchen is essential for peace of mind and retirement.

This book does three things: First, it provides a game plan that works in any negotiation situation. I dispel the faulty belief that negotiations in boardrooms or real estate deals are fundamentally different from salary negotiations, school and community negotiation, and, yes, negotiations with spouses and kids. Chances are, if you are great at making real estate deals, then you also will be great at negotiating with a caterer for your local charity's fundraiser.

Second, this book focuses on the two key tasks of any negotiation: creating win–win deals by leveraging information carefully collected from the other party and effectively laying claim to part of the win–win goldmine.

Finally, this book talks about how to handle less-than-perfect situations, such as when you make a threat (that you did not really mean), how to establish trust with someone you don't trust, how to walk away at the right time, and how to negotiate with people you don't really like and, at the other end of the spectrum, people you love very much.

Negotiation may sound daunting, but if you are informed, practiced, and prepared, even you can do it. And that's the truth.

PART I
NEGOTIATION:
A 30,000-FOOT VIEW

Before we start cracking the negotiation code that is present in all of our interactions—with our boss, spouse, neighbor, and attorney—it is important to look at the big picture of negotiation. First and foremost, anyone with the will to learn and improve has the potential to become a world-class negotiator.

TRUTH

1

Negotiation:
A natural gift?

I have never met a natural-born negotiator. The best negotiators I've met have been self-made, not manufactured by their parents. People can adapt and improve with conscious effort, and, in fact, that is the only path to becoming a good negotiator. Your ability to do well in life's most important negotiations isn't determined by your basic personality or genetic structure. It's most strongly determined by a simple factor: your motivation to improve.

Nevertheless, a great number of people believe successful negotiation is all in the DNA and that negotiation, like good looks, is something you're born with.

You don't have to travel far to see that the right kind of experience can dramatically improve your negotiation outcomes. The "magic bullet," when it comes to experiences that enhance negotiation skills, is the I–C–E rule:

- *Immediate* feedback (preferably within one hour)
- *Clarity* about useful (and useless) behaviors
- *Empirically* tested best practices (that don't require a lot of time and expense)

Negotiation is something you can practice and improve upon. For example, suppose that, if, immediately after a negotiation (within 20 minutes), someone would evaluate your performance, analyze your behaviors, and then give you a toolbox to ensure that you didn't repeat mistakes. Your negotiation skills would undoubtedly improve. For example, when I've put this very model to the test in research and classrooms, people's performance usually improves dramatically—by over 20 percent on average. So, the question is how can most of us significantly improve our ability to negotiate in our day-to-day negotiations? How can we become our own best teacher and our best student?

> The best negotiators I've met have been self-made, not manufactured by their parents.

As you read this book, I suggest that you follow the advice given to the person who asked how to get to Carnegie Hall: "Practice." Test the skills of each Truth and, if possible, get prompt, clear feedback. The more time and effort you put into trying out the various points and techniques shared, the more prepared you will be.

TRUTH

2

The magic bullet:
Preparation

Most people look for a magic bullet when it comes to negotiation, and, well, there is one. Are you ready? Okay, here it is: Prepare. After years of offering this advice, sending people off, and expecting magic to occur that never did, I finally realized the problem: Rehearsing does not equal preparation.

There are two styles of preparation, and only one of them works. Let's call the two styles Pattern X and Pattern Y.

Pattern X Preparation

These activities seem to be useful but aren't:

- Rehearsing your demands
- Pumping yourself up
- Making a personal pledge to yourself or your partner to act tough
- Figuring out how to derail the other negotiators or make them feel uncomfortable, which includes rearranging furniture, deliberately arriving late, and making them face glaring light
- Preparing backhanded compliments and outright insults
- Rehearsing phrases such as "This is my final offer"; "My bottom line"; "This is a deal-breaker"; "Nonnegotiable"; and "Then we don't have a deal"
- Framing your opening offer as a demand

Pattern Y Preparation

These activities are extraordinarily useful, but negotiators often don't engage in them:

- Brainstorming all issues under consideration (for example, payment, terms and conditions, indemnities, volume, distribution)
- Arranging those issues in order of importance or priority to you (either by using a simple rank order or allocating 100 points among the issues to reflect what percentage of overall importance each represents)
- For each issue, brainstorming all the alternatives (for example, payment terms might range from 0 percent to paid-in-full)

- Brainstorming issues the other party might care about
- Identifying your most desirable set of terms for each of the issues
- Identifying and prioritizing your alternative courses of action to negotiating with this person (for example, liquidating your product)
- Identifying the other party's potential alternative courses of action
- Preparing an opening offer

> Pattern Y negotiators have measurably better outcomes than do Pattern X negotiators.

If negotiators did even a subset of these activities to prepare for a negotiation, they would fare dramatically better than if they didn't. In other words, Pattern Y negotiators have measurably better outcomes than do Pattern X negotiators. Pattern X is more likely to strike out; Pattern Y gets you to yes.

The question, then, is how to get people to follow Pattern Y when most of them are used to Pattern X. Clearly, relying on natural instinct won't work. So let me suggest that you use a strategy I call *guided preparation*. If unguided preparation is allowing negotiators to do whatever they want, guided preparation is giving them a step-by-step method to follow. Professor Jeanne Brett at the Kellogg School of Management devised an easy-to-follow model that you can use with a single sheet of paper divided into three columns:

1. List all the issues to be negotiated in the first column. (Be ready to add issues the other party mentions.)

2. For each of the issues listed, in the second column, indicate its relative importance to you (by rank ordering or allocating 100 points among the issues), your most desired terms, and your underlying interests.

3. For all issues, in the third column make your best guess about the counterparty's interests, rankings, and most desired terms.

If you have accomplished these three things, you can get some sleep, knowing you have prepared effectively.

3

Your industry is unique (and other myths)

Contrary to popular thought, the basic structure of negotiation does not differ that much across different industries.

Myth #1: Your industry is unique

No matter what the industry, negotiators have specific issues that are important to them. For example, a home buyer might focus on price, closing date, and financing terms. A sales manager might focus on price, volume, and rebates. The key thing for both of these negotiators is not the nuances of how closing dates and royalty rates work but rather the fact that they both care about certain issues and may or may not be willing to make concessions in regard to them. Similarly, both a home buyer and a sales manager might have a "bottom line" and might be inclined to make threats. The parallels between negotiations in different industries far outnumber any differences.

Here's an analogy. Suppose your child said, "I really want to learn how to play card games, and I need to know 'card math.' Can you teach me?" Later that evening, your child says, "Can you please teach me basketball math to figure out players' stats?" Then at bedtime, "I have to figure out how to do candy math so when I buy candy I can count the change."

You'd probably say, "I have good news: There's no difference between card math, basketball math, and candy math. For that matter, there's no difference between grocery store math, checkbook math, and dessert math. Math is math. There are certain key rules and operators you can use whether you're playing poker, analyzing basketball stats, or buying lollipops. Once you know the rules, you can use them anywhere."

Negotiation is negotiation. Scientific principles apply to all of life's negotiations, from the most

> You can use the same principles to negotiate with a loan officer that you can with a colleague or spouse.

intimate to the most economic. In other words, you can use the same principles to negotiate with a loan officer that you can with a colleague or spouse.

The fact that all negotiations (whether with nannies or Wall Street financiers) have predictable parallels is good news. Why? It means there's a science to negotiation, and once we crack the code, we can use our skills any time with anyone.

> There's a science to negotiation, and once we crack the code, we can use our skills any time with anyone.

Also, you may begin a career in consulting, change to insurance, and then end up in the public sector. Because of the parallels among negotiation types, you won't have to reinvent yourself each time—at least as a negotiator.

There are three more myths I want to clear up so that we're on the same page.

Myth #2: Business people care only about money

This is false. Business people seek to maximize their utility. So do professors, students, home buyers, parents, children, spouses, and professional wrestlers. Your utility is not your money. Your utility represents your overall satisfaction with a particular situation. When I negotiate with my child or someone else I care about, I want him to be happy, too. So his happiness is part of my utility, and in my negotiations with him, I am seeking to maximize my utility, which includes my welfare and his. Excellent salespeople know that customers are valuable, so part of their own utility is pleasing the customer.

Myth #3: Always maintain a poker face: Never reveal anything

This is false, too. Negotiators who fail to reveal anything are doomed to lose–lose agreements.

Myth #4: Never make the first offer

Again, this one's false. There isn't a single published scientific investigation that supports this advice in any way. I challenge you to find any scientific evidence that does. In fact, many studies support the wisdom of making the first offer.

TRUTH

4

Win–win, win–lose, and lose–lose negotiations

Management guru Mary Parker Follett tells a story of two sisters quarreling over a single orange. Both sisters want the orange, and they are willing to fight for it. They state their demands, and the negotiation escalates. Battle weary, the sisters finally agree to compromise and cut the orange exactly in half. One sister squeezes the juice from her half to make fresh orange juice and discards the peel. The other sister grates her half of the peel for an orange scone recipe and throws out the juice. The garbage truck comes and goes with the discarded remains....

In the heat of the argument, the sisters overlooked a simple win–win solution: One sister would get the whole peel, the other all the juice. Tragically, by the time the sisters realized their error, the fruit's remains were gone. By acting purely competitively, the "Orange Sisters" turned an easy win–win into a lose–lose negotiation. Why? The sisters made demands and stated positions but failed to communicate their interests.

Most negotiations contain potential for win–win agreements. For example, had the sisters been willing to reveal what their goals, interests, and intentions were, they might have discovered the win–win solution of giving the entire peel to one sister and all the juice to the other.

Win–win negotiation is the process of crafting arrangements that represent mutual gains for all parties involved. Win–win deals involve both creating value and claiming value. To create value, we need to cooperate with the other party and genuinely work with their interests in mind. For example, the sisters needed to find it in themselves to ask questions and gain insight about why each needed the orange.

When it comes to claiming value, no one wants to get no part of the orange or just a sliver. For this reason, each negotiator must be her own best advocate. And, so, it's necessary to make claims in a negotiation. But making claims is different from making demands. Claiming value, then, refers to how negotiators garner resources for themselves and their companies. It's possible to be both competitive and cooperative in a negotiation: competitive about looking after your own interests but cooperative in terms of exploring creative options.

Too often, I see negotiators make one of two mistakes: They either concede too quickly—accommodate excessively—or act too tough. Both mistakes can result in win–lose outcomes or lose–lose outcomes.

Win–win negotiation

A true win–win negotiation is a solution in which parties have reached an agreement that cannot be mutually improved upon. Had the sisters come up with the elegant solution of giving the entire peel to one and the entire fruit to the other, this would have been win–win. The term *win–win negotiation* actually reflects an important economic concept: Win–win solutions lie on what economists refer to as the Pareto Optimal Frontier, after the Italian economist Vilfredo Pareto.

> A true win–win negotiation is a solution in which parties have reached an agreement that cannot be mutually improved upon.

Lose–lose negotiation

Pareto's litmus test was simple: If there is no way to improve upon an agreement from the standpoint of either party, the negotiators have reached the Pareto Optimal Frontier. However, if there is another agreement that both parties would prefer or that one party prefers and the other is indifferent to, the negotiators have suboptimized, failing to reach the Pareto Optimal Frontier. When this happens, I call it a *lose–lose agreement*.

These are the tell-tale signs of a lose–lose negotiation:

- The other party immediately accepted your first offer.
- You made an offer, the other party counteroffered, and then you agreed to split the difference.
- You and the other party considered fewer than five potential deals.
- You didn't ask the other party any questions.
- The other party didn't ask you any questions.
- Neither party tried to "tweak" the deal to improve it.

- You revealed nothing to the other party.
- The other party revealed nothing to you.
- You negotiated only one issue (such as price).
- You negotiated more than one issue, but you negotiated each independently of the others.

If your negotiation is characterized by three or more of these symptoms, there is a very good chance you suboptimized and ended up with a lose–lose deal. Fortunately, you can do several things to make sure you never end up on the "lose–lose frontier" again.

Win–lose negotiation

Win–lose negotiations happen when one party makes all the concessions and the other party makes excessive demands. In the orange example, imagine if one sister had been tougher than the other. The tough sister would have gotten the entire orange for herself, and the concessionary sister would have not gotten anything. We call this win–lose negotiation. Win–lose negotiators create problems in long-term relationships because parties often want to get even or hold a grudge.

Negotiators struggle with the question of whether to be tough and demanding or nice and conciliatory. "Do I want to succeed, or do I want to build relationships?"

Sometimes negotiators opt to make concessions and sacrifices because they want the other party to like and trust them, and frankly it's just more comfortable. The downside: These negotiators perform less well economically.

In this book, we move away from the stark choice of being tough versus being soft. Tough, unrelenting negotiators risk not making deals at all (lose–lose), or they may win this one but leave the other party feeling embittered and resentful (win–lose).

TRUTH

5

Four sand traps in the golf game of negotiation

My dad has been a golfer for as long as I can remember. He had a golf analogy for almost every aspect of life. The first time he took me golfing, I hit the ball straight into the first hole's sand trap. "Is that good, Dad?" "No, it's not. It's hard to get out of there. You need to stay OUT of the sand traps in the first place."

When I started seeing patterns in the underperformance of otherwise smart people at the negotiation table, it occurred to me to think of these problems as sand traps. Every negotiation table is like a golf course: We may not have played a particular course before, but all courses have sand traps, and it helps to know where they are. If we know where the problem spots are, we're in a better position to reach our goals. If we hit our ball into a marsh on the first hole, we may never recover.

This Truth outlines four sand traps. I've been in every one of them, and I'd sure like to see you avoid them.

Sand trap #1: Leaving money on the table

Leaving money on the table is a lose–lose negotiation. Lose–lose negotiation, not surprisingly, is the opposite of win–win. On average, people settle for terms worse for both parties in one out of every five negotiations![1] The problem is that they are unaware that win–win possibilities exist.

Sand trap #2: Settling for too little

This is also known as the *winner's curse*. Consider Ron, for example, who was in Kuwait during the Gulf War. During his time of service, Ron was engaged, and he wanted to buy his fiancée a gold necklace before he returned to the States. He spotted the perfect necklace in a Kuwait jewelry store. It was priced at about $600 U.S. dollars. Ron offered the merchant $300. "Sold!" the merchant said immediately, beaming. Ron was proud of his ability to get such a great deal. But the merchant was giddily happy and even offered Ron a free matching set of earrings. Ron's pride turned into regret. He had fallen prey to the winner's curse, which occurs when a negotiator's first proposal is immediately accepted by the other party, signaling that the offer was too generous.

When Ron realized he had fallen prey to the winner's curse, he couldn't easily retract his offer in good faith. The merchant had already packed the necklace and earrings in a charming gift box and embraced Ron, wishing him "a wonderful married life!"

Sand trap #3: Walking away from the table

This is the "hubris" problem. Negotiators who are so prideful that they walk away from the table dramatically even when they have no other attractive options are essentially bluffing. They lack the good sense to swallow their pride and return to the table.

I have known several negotiators guilty of hubris. They often dig their own graves because once they have made a take-it-or-leave-it offer, they can't tolerate the thought of losing face by returning to the table. You may argue that it's important to display toughness and resolve to the other side. However, earning a reputation for being tough doesn't serve you well at the negotiation table. Indeed, a reputation as a tough negotiator leads to a number of highly undesirable outcomes—for example, counterparties will treat you with greater suspicion and act much tougher than they normally would. In an investigation of how bargaining reputation affects how others treat you, Cathy Tinsley found that "tough guys finish last," meaning that people negotiate more aggressively with those who have a reputation for toughness.[2]

Sand trap #4: Settling for terms that are worse than your current situation

I call this the "agreement bias." I use it to refer to the negotiator who is so desperate to make a deal that she literally forgets she has a better alternative elsewhere and accepts the offer in the heat of the moment.

For example, if I currently have an offer of $300,000 for my home and your best offer to me is $295,000, it wouldn't be in my interest to make a deal with you, all other things being equal.

Nevertheless, negotiators often get swept away by a negotiation's momentum. Indeed, once we sit down at the table and invest in a relationship, we often feel bad walking away from it. Simply put, negotiators often rationalize accepting inferior terms.

To prevent this, write your walk-away point on a piece of paper so you can refer to it before you accept a proposal. Obviously, the writing should be encrypted so that the note wouldn't mean much more than a grocery shopping list if the other party sees it!

Write your walk-away point on a piece of paper so you can refer to it before you accept a proposal.

TRUTH

6

If you have only one hour to prepare…

Negotiation does not just occur in used car lots, boardrooms, or lawyers' offices. You negotiate every day: with your spouse to split up household tasks, with your colleagues regarding who will take a client's call, with your kids to determine the best time for bed or for curfew....Any time meeting your goals requires the cooperation of others, you must negotiate.

Sometimes you have significant time to prepare for a negotiation. But other times you get blindsided: You get a call from an old friend with a "hot" business opportunity. Or you receive a disturbing email from a colleague, claiming resources you believe to be yours. Or your nanny or assistant threatens to leave unless you give her a raise and a three-week vacation. In all these situations, you may feel there's no time to prepare for negotiation.

But even if you've got only an hour—or just moments—to prepare, there are several crucial steps you have to take.

> Any time meeting your goals requires the cooperation of others, you must negotiate.

1. Identify your real goals.
2. Brainstorm your options.
3. Plan your opening move.

Identify your goals

Negotiators are often quick to stake out a position. A position is a demand, such as, "I want a bonus!" The danger in stating a position is that it can lead the other party to stake out a position, such as, "No way; I'm not paying you a bonus!"

Conversely, negotiators who move past positions to focus on their interests usually achieve their goals. A real goal reflects a negotiator's interests and answers the "why" question. Take the case of two colleagues negotiating who gets the more spacious office in a suite. It would be easy for both colleagues to say, "I want the bigger office." That is a demand. If the colleagues articulate why they desire the bigger office, they are getting closer to stating their goals. For example, one colleague might want the larger office because it would allow her to have team meetings that are currently impossible to schedule in a conference room, and she is under pressure to deliver on a deadline. The other colleague might want the office to impress important clients.

People's demands may be incompatible, but their goals might be compatible or at least complementary.

People's demands may be incompatible, but their goals might be compatible or at least complementary. For example, if the two colleagues articulate their goals, they might create an arrangement in which they share the big office, reserving it for meetings with clients.

Brainstorm your options

Negotiations do not always end in mutual settlement. A colleague may pull rank to acquire the big office; the nanny may quit; the company may not take your offer. So you need to face the thorny question of what you will do in the absence of agreement. In short, what are your alternative courses of action? Most people have tunnel vision when it comes to their alternative courses of action in a negotiation. They are so focused on their demands that they can't see all the different paths through the forest. Identify your options using the four fundamental rules of brainstorming:[3]

- Suspend your initial judgment and just list all options that come to mind, even outlandish ones.

- Strive for quantity; often, a good idea emerges from several silly-sounding ones.

- Reserve judgment and evaluation until later.

- Mix, match, and combine different options.

Plan your opening move

Your opening offer should clearly articulate your goal and suggest how to reach it. ("I would like the corner office because my client load is highest in the office, and my team is unable to fit in the current space.") You don't need to blurt out your opening offer the moment you meet with the other party. But, at some point, after you exchange pleasantries, it will be your turn to anchor the negotiation. Your opening offer should represent the ideal situation for you. State it clearly but do not position your offer as a demand. One direct but nondemanding way of doing this is, "In the spirit of getting the discussion started, I've mapped out a set of terms that works for me.…" Another is, "I want to respect your time, so I have prepared a proposal that I would like to get your reaction to.…"

Be firm about your interests but flexible on how to achieve them. Don't make take-it-or-leave-it demands. If you are feeling demanding or indignant before the negotiation, prepare an opening that you might present to someone you care about (such as your spouse or friend)—even if you don't particularly care about the other party. The danger of making insulting, take-it-or-leave-it offers is that most people will opt to leave it.

PART 2
THE BOTTOM LINE ON BOTTOM LINES

Your bottom line is everything in a negotiation. However, most people don't know how to accurately determine their bottom line and, most importantly, how to leverage it to their advantage.

TRUTH

7

Identify your BATNA

When our sons were ages 10 and 11, my husband and I made a grave mistake in mindlessly allowing both boys to sign up for travel basketball teams. At the time, I did not appreciate the literal meaning of the word travel, but I found out quickly that for 10 weekends in a row, the entire family would be on the road and sitting in smelly gyms across the greater Midwest! Moreover, because these youth games start at the ungodly hour of 8 a.m., it became necessary to spend the night in a hotel the night before. Thus, our hotel bills started to mount perilously high.

On one occasion, the entire team had to travel to Wisconsin for two nights. Once I realized that all the families on the team were in the same position as we were, I recognized that I was in a potentially powerful negotiation position to negotiate blocks of rooms with hotels.

So, I started my research. I made an Excel list of all the hotels within a 10-mile radius of the gym. At the top of my list was a Holiday Inn that had a kids' water park. (None of the other nearby hotels had such a perk, so this was clearly my first choice.) I called the events manager and asked about getting a good rate for this block of rooms. Normally, the room rates were well above $200 a night.

When I found the Holiday Inn with the water park, I already had a fallback option, but not an attractive one. The Comfort Inn was not as nice as the Holiday Inn, but it was cheap. Yet, it had no "kid appeal" (which potentially meant that parents would be forced to do all the entertaining). The Comfort Inn was my best alternative to negotiating an agreement with the Holiday Inn. The Comfort Inn, therefore, was my best alternative to a negotiated agreement—my BATNA![4] Having a BATNA helped me to leverage my power in the negotiation with the Holiday Inn, where we got a very good rate.

* * *

Some time ago, a friend came to me to seek advice. Our conversation went something like this:

> Friend: "I'm glad Company X made me an offer, but the offer isn't that great. I want a higher salary, better benefits, a signing bonus, and moving expenses. My friends are all getting those."

Me: "What will you do if they don't improve the offer?"

Friend: "What do you mean?"

Me: "How many other job offers do you have?"

Friend: "Just this one. But it's a good company!"

Me: "Have you ever heard of a BATNA? Your key source of power in a negotiation is your ability to walk away, which depends on your BATNA. It's the power of alternatives."

Friend: "I don't have a BATNA!" *(panicking)*

Me: "Calm down. You do have a BATNA. You always have a BATNA. What you're saying is that you don't *like* your BATNA. It's unattractive to you. But you have one."

What I mean by "You always have a BATNA" is that you will always do something if you fail to reach an agreement with the other party, even if it means becoming jobless, homeless, or bankrupt. Of course, those are extreme cases. In most negotiations, people have a few alternatives that may not be ideal, but they're tolerable.

> "You always have a BATNA. What you're saying is that you don't like your BATNA. It's unattractive to you. But you have one."

To get back to the friend: His BATNA was to extend his job search indefinitely. He chose not to accept Company X's offer because he was optimistic that some Company Y would eventually make him a better offer.

Similarly, a home seller may reject a lowball offer from an uncooperative buyer in the hope that the future will bring a better offer.

Finally, to return to hotel negotiation: If my negotiations with the Holiday Inn had not resulted in an offer that was more attractive than what the Comfort Inn offered me, I would have walked away from the table.

TRUTH

8

Develop your reservation price

A few years ago, I was selling my house. I tried to practice what I preach in my classes: Develop an attractive BATNA, set a feasible target (aspiration point), and so on. But none of it changed the hard truth that I didn't have an offer on my house!

To make matters worse, I made the grave mistake of telling friends about my lack of success. From that point, they took daily delight in grilling me about the house: "Hey, what's your BATNA?" As the days dragged on and I still didn't have an offer, I'd hear things like, "I can loan you a good book!"

One day I arrived at work with a picture of drunken fraternity guys on my laptop screen. They were surrounded by empty bottles and other party paraphernalia. A murmur rippled through the office. Had I forgotten to change my screen saver after a wild spring break? Was I having a midlife crisis?

"Here's my BATNA," I announced solemnly. Blank looks. I explained that in the event that I didn't get an offer on my house, my next best course of action would be to rent it—to these party animals. I described the men in the picture as undergraduates taking all of their courses pass/fail. My coworkers were concerned: "Wouldn't these 'young men' destroy your house?" This led to a discussion about risk and the benefits of a damage deposit. Then more questions: "Are these guys going to agree to let you have realtors show the house?" That led to a discussion of the wisdom of securing a contractual agreement that would involve a clear understanding of certain hours during which the house could be shown. Then more discussion, about neighbors growing angry with loud music from the house, my name on the police blotter, and the like.

Finally, someone said, "So what's the least money I could offer you for your house now where you would be indifferent between the party animals and my offer?" In short, what is the monetary equivalent of my BATNA? In other words, even though BATNAs, just like the party animals, are messy, subjective, and psychological, we must be able to make them monetary; otherwise, we won't be able to compare alternatives meaningfully.

Given that I put a value on subjective-emotional things such as my time, peace of mind, marital harmony, neighborly relations, liquid assets, and absence of conflicts, I came up with a number. A penny less meant that I would rather rent than sell. A penny more meant that I would rather sell than rent. That indifference point is my reservation price. It's what negotiators mean by their "bottom line."

A different person selling the same house with my same BATNA might have a different reservation point because he or she has a different value system, different risk psychology, and so on.

Thus, the beauty of a reservation point is that it quantifies subjective values.

The lesson: After you identify your BATNA, convert it to a reservation point.

Recall my friend who was looking for a job. Say that he determined the least amount of money that Company X could offer him such that he would be indifferent to accepting the offer versus declining it and extending his job search. That go-no-go number would be his reservation point.

9

It's alive! Constantly improve your BATNA

> Think of your BATNA as a beloved plant or pet: You feed it, you water it. BATNAs need care and attention to thrive. If you stop nurturing them, they die.

Your BATNA is in a constant state of flux. It ebbs and flows. Whatever you do, don't be passive about it. For example, a home buyer might have three offers on her house today. Great BATNA, you might think. But three days from now, the inspection may go badly for one buyer, another buyer may not get the company transfer he anticipated and withdraw, and the third may find a more attractive house. So, now the seller's BATNAs have withered. In this situation, I would advise the seller to schedule an open house, create a colorful website, and move ahead with a touch-up paint job. Even if a seller has three offers in hand, it's wise to keep playing the field until the deal is signed, sealed, and delivered.

I've seen too many negotiators release their BATNAs before the proverbial cat is in the proverbial bag. A home buyer might fall in love with the second house she sees and refuse to view any others. A job recruiter might cancel all remaining interviews once the first candidate meets the bar. Prematurely releasing your BATNA dramatically reduces your power.

The surest way to improve your outcome and leverage your power better in any negotiation is to increase your BATNA's attractiveness. For example, a job seeker might attempt to garner two or three job offers. Similarly, a new car buyer might pit several sellers against one another, asking each to meet or beat the others' prices.

Having said this, I do not advocate starting bidding wars. Negotiators who use their BATNAs in a threatening fashion create ill will. What to do instead? First, list your options in order of attractiveness. Suppose you're a job candidate, and four companies have made you offers: Company W, Company X, Company Y, and Company Z. So far, you like Company W the most, but the other options are close behind. As tempting as it may be to start a bidding war, I would avoid it. Rather, I advise approaching Company W and saying something like:

I do not advocate starting bidding wars.

If you give me an offer that has A, B, and C in it, I will accept immediately without asking for anything else. But if you're unable to offer me these terms, I'll need more time to decide. Please understand that I would still be interested in the offer and may decide to accept it.

What I like about this strategy is that the counterparty is reassured that you are not going to start a bidding war and that she can close the deal right now with you.

The best way of improving your BATNA is to fully explore all possible courses of action.

For example, think back to the friend who had the suboptimal job offer from Company X. He might list his alternatives as follows:

- Continue the job search. (I learned that my friend had second-round interviews at two companies, was short-listed at three more, and had other interviews scheduled. Based on this, he figured there was an 80 percent chance he'd have a job offer from another company within three weeks.)

- Work as an intern, temp, or research assistant. (He had a written invitation from an accounting professor to work on a short-term project that was not high paying but was rewarding and prestigious.)

- Flip burgers. (This may sound like a joke, but everyone should be open to several courses of action.)

The friend ranked his alternatives in order of attractiveness (utility to him). Of all the options, he was most keen about extending his formal job search and decided to focus on his upcoming job interviews.

Skilled negotiators always keep their alternatives open and attempt to improve upon them.

TRUTH

10

Don't reveal your BATNA

"Why is it so bad to reveal my BATNA?" you may ask. Once you reveal your BATNA, the other party has no incentive to offer you any more than your BATNA. Consider the following scenario:

> Home seller: "My house is listed at $250,000. Another buyer has made an offer, but it's only for $175,000, which is too low. I'd like you to offer something in the range of $225,000 to $240,000."

> Homebuyer: "Your house is lovely. However, I have my own financial needs to consider. I'll make you a cash offer of $176,000, and we can close at your convenience."

If you sensed something wrong with the home seller's approach, you're right: The seller revealed the BATNA to the other party. What's more, the BATNA was relatively unattractive. Once the homebuyer knows this information, she has absolutely no incentive to offer the seller anything but the bare minimum over the seller's BATNA, as illustrated in this example. Once you reveal your BATNA, the counterparty has you over a barrel.

Rest assured that other parties will seek information about your BATNA in a million different ways. They will prod you, quiz you, and taunt you. It's best to think of yourself as a CIA agent who has taken an oath never to reveal your BATNA, lest it compromise the nation's security.

> Think of yourself as a CIA agent who has taken an oath never to reveal your BATNA, lest it compromise the nation's security.

Are there special cases in which it makes sense to reveal your BATNA? I can think of only two:

- The eleventh hour is at hand, and negotiations are at a standstill. You've spent all day negotiating and gotten nowhere. If you don't reach an agreement, you'll miss your flight home. Before you walk out the door, you might consider revealing your BATNA. There's a chance the other party may meet it or beat it.

- You have a fantastic BATNA and would be happy simply to have the counterparty match or trivially improve upon it. But if you choose to reveal your BATNA, understand one thing: You're not going to get an offer significantly more attractive than it from any rational other party.

These situations are truly rare. If you're like me, you don't want the other party to simply meet your BATNA—you want him to think it's much more attractive than it really is, so he'll make you a much better offer. So, don't share your BATNA unless you absolutely have to. And, even then, proceed carefully.

TRUTH

11

Don't lie about your BATNA

Your BATNA is your key source of bargaining power. And I've strictly cautioned you against revealing your BATNA. These may add up to a common temptation: Why not lie about your BATNA to claim a larger slice of the bargaining pie?

For instance, suppose I concoct a plan for getting a hefty raise: I plan to tell my boss that I have an amazing offer from another employer (this is a complete lie) and that to keep me, she must meet or beat it. Now, you try to talk me out of this deceitful plan!

You might try to talk me out of this plan by saying, "You'll surely ruin your reputation if you lie. It's a small world, and your boss will probably find out that you're lying. She'll never trust you again. You'll lose all respect at work." "Isn't it important to have some integrity?" "How would you like it if someone lied to you that way? Wouldn't you want to fire him?"

Okay, I'm beginning to see the light. Trying to bilk my boss sounds like a stinker of an idea from this ethical standpoint.

Are there any more reasons not to carry out my plan?

You might say, "Suppose your boss calls your bluff and says, 'Congratulations on the offer. We're proud of you and will miss you. I'm sure you'll enjoy your new job.'"

Oh dear, you're right again. If I lie about my BATNA, the counterparty might call my bluff, and then I would have one heck of a face-saving act to perform: "Uh, well, boss, I haven't quite decided to take the offer, and come to think of it, my kids really like the schools here…and I don't want to go through the trauma of a move. So never mind."

Okay, you've almost convinced me not to lie. Any additional arguments?

At this point, you say, "Are you aware that lying about a material fact is prosecutable?" You show me the legal code on this and explain that if my boss enters into an agreement based upon a material fact that I have knowingly misrepresented, I can be sued.

In sum, there are three darn good reasons to never lie about your BATNA:

- **Ethical/moral**—You don't want to behave this way because it implicitly encourages others to behave similarly, which creates a corrupt society. Plus you'll ruin your reputation.

- **Strategic face-saving**—Just as in poker, someone can call your bluff at any time. In negotiation, there are many more "tells," or signs that someone's lying.

> Just as in poker, someone can call your bluff at any time.

- **Legal/contractual**—Lying about a material fact (such as claiming that you have another job offer or an offer on your house that you do not in fact possess) is a criminal act that may result in prosecution or a lawsuit.

TRUTH

12

Signal your BATNA

You may have noticed a BATNA-related Catch-22: "I can't tell the truth without being totally duped, and I can't lie without suffering moral-strategic-legal costs. What exactly do you advise?"

To make matters worse, counterparties often ask you about your BATNA directly. "Do you have any offers yet?" Similarly, a homebuyer asks home sellers, "Any action on your home?" And a vendor might bait a procurement director with, "Do you have another source for this product?"

So, what should you do when hit with a "What's-your-BATNA" question?

First, there are two things you shouldn't do:

- Don't ignore the question and hope it will go away. It won't.
- Don't turn the question around by saying, "I'll show you mine if you show me yours."

Rather, signal to the other party that you have a BATNA, without revealing it: "If you're inquiring about whether I have alternative courses of action, the answer is yes. But I'm sure you can understand why I can't discuss those with you at this time."

> Signal to the other party that you have a BATNA, without revealing it.

Here's another strategy that I like even better, in the context of an interested company asking a job-seeker how many job offers she has: "I put an 80 percent probability on my having an offer from a Fortune 100 firm in the next two weeks. I have three second-round interviews. I am on the short list at eight companies. And I have two phone interviews this week and five recruiting events coming up."

Reading between the lines, it's clear that this job-seeker does not have another job offer in hand, but she is signaling that her BATNA is being actively watered and fertilized and is blossoming wildly. Of course, I advocate saying these things only if they're true. This again points out the importance of not releasing your alternatives prematurely. Even if you get a tempting job offer, keep interviewing and attending recruiting events!

The good thing about signaling is that saying things like, "I put an X percent chance on event Y happening" is not a material fact. It is a subjective probability.

Don't signal your BATNA to threaten the other party. Rather, send signals under the following conditions:

■ The counterparty challenges you directly. ("Do you have any other job offers?")

■ The counterparty severely underestimates your alternatives.

■ The counterparty has faulty information about you that you want to set straight.

■ The counterparty low-balled you, and you wish to signal that he needs to increase the value of his proposals quickly.

TRUTH

13

Research the other party's BATNA

If your feet are the key source of your bargaining power in a negotiation, bear in mind that the other party has feet, too.

It's surprising to me how little research negotiators do on the other party. Negotiators become so self-absorbed with their own BATNAs that they often fail to think strategically about who's on the other side of the table. This is even more perplexing when there is good data available, often publicly, about the other party.

In my first job, I was earning a rather low salary. "It's okay....I'm doing what really counts," I would tell myself. Fortunately, a fellow employee hinted to me that I might be underpaid. Salaries are a matter of public information at state and federal jobs. So I went to the library and spent several hours finding out exactly what everyone was paid. Then I did some further analysis of salaries based on gender, years of experience, field of study, and so on. Using the information, I made charts and graphs and plotted myself on them among several comparison points including performance. Then I made an appointment with my boss. I got a raise in less than two weeks.

If you don't research your case, you may falsely assume that the other party's BATNA is better than it is, which puts you in a position of weakness. Moreover, if you focus just on your own BATNA, you get anchored by it. Even if you don't uncover relevant data about the other party's BATNA, thinking about the other person's BATNA dramatically improves your outcome.[5]

Here are the big five DO's and DON'Ts when it comes to BATNAs:

- DON'T reveal your BATNA, except under special conditions.
- DO as much research as possible on the other party's BATNA.
- DON'T engage in bidding wars but, DO make constant attempts to improve your BATNA.
- DON'T lie about your BATNA.
- DO signal to the other party that you have valuable alternative options.

PART 3
BLACK BELT
NEGOTIATION SKILLS

You've prepared your bottom line. You've thought about theirs. Now you are in the throes. What should you reveal? What should you conceal? Should you open first? How can you craft a win–win deal without risking giving up too much?

TRUTH

14

Set optimistic but realistic aspirations

While having a best alternative to a negotiated agreement (BATNA) is important, there is a risk that you could become so focused on your BATNA and reservation point that you would settle for the first deal better than your BATNA or above your reservation point. Instead, you should hold out for a much more attractive deal, one closer to your aspiration point.

Your BATNA tells you when to *walk*, not when to *sign*.

> Your BATNA tells you when to *walk*, not when to *sign*.

If you accept the first proposal that exceeds your BATNA, you have fallen victim to the "underaspiring" negotiator syndrome. The primary symptom: You feel lucky just to have reached an agreement. However, when you later discover that the bargaining zone—the distance between both parties' reservation prices—was much larger than you realized, your excitement may melt into disappointment.

What you need is an *aspiration point*. An aspiration point represents the monetary equivalent of your ideal set of terms. Suppose you are selling your house. You might tell me your reservation price is $250,000 (and your house is listed at $275,000). I would ask you if that represents a favorable set of terms. I want you to be optimistic but realistic. You may say then that $275,000 would be attractive and realistic because that's what comparable houses have sold for in your neighborhood. That's your aspiration point! The person you negotiate with will have, whether she knows it or not, an aspiration point, too. That's why it's important that you know yours.

You need to develop your aspiration point *before* going into negotiation. It's not enough to simply hope to secure an agreement that is better than your BATNA. I'm also not a fan of aspiration "ranges." Ranges are wishy-washy; they have diminished anchoring potential and, not surprisingly, the counterparty tends to hear only the part of your range closest to *her* aspiration point (the lowest price you're willing to sell for). So, it's essential to develop an actual aspiration point—I call it a *target*—for the negotiation. Not to have and to know your aspiration point is like going into a negotiation with a defense but no offense.

But you can also go too far with your aspirations. You could develop wildly unrealistic aspiration points. The danger of developing an outlandish target is that it can create the *chilling effect* in the counterparty and set you up for disappointment.

The chilling effect occurs when an opening offer is so insulting that the counterparty doesn't even care to respond because he doesn't want to acknowledge it. Suppose, for example, that a buyer makes a $100,000 offer on your $275,000 home. You wouldn't even want to give that buyer the courtesy of a response. That's the chilling effect. The polar opposite of the chilling effect is the *winner's curse*. If you immediately and gleefully accept my first offer, that tells me my offer was too generous. You should not accept the first offer above your reservation price.

> Suppose, for example, that a buyer makes a $100,000 offer on your $275,000 home. You wouldn't even want to give that buyer the courtesy of a response. That's the chilling effect.

Here are the aspiration point DOs:

■ DO think about the other party's BATNA. You don't know what it is, of course, but you can still think about it. As it turns out, if you were to develop an aspiration point that was exactly equivalent to the other party's BATNA/reservation point, that would be a great opening offer to make.

■ DO seek comparison data and focus on points that are most favorable to you (as you would do if you researched the salaries or fees earned by people with similar qualifications and experience to yours).

■ DO follow these basic steps:

1. Identify your key goals.

2. Brainstorm your options.

3. Plan your opening move.

Your aspiration should be such that if you proposed your terms and the other party immediately accepted, you would still feel good.

Here are the DON'Ts:

- DON'T use your BATNA as a starting point and then dial it up or down to arrive at a target point. You can't derive your aspiration from a BATNA-based formula.

- DON'T state an outrageous aspiration that you can't back up with data, facts, and logic.

- DON'T withhold your aspiration until the other party has spoken.

- DON'T state a range of aspiration points.

TRUTH

15

The power of making the first offer

Conventional negotiation wisdom strictly cautions negotiators against opening first—to avoid tipping their hands. If everyone does this, you are liable to end up in a comical cat-and-mouse game in which both parties develop elaborate methods to avoid answering any questions as long as possible and eventually walk away without a deal.

I don't know the origin of this bad advice, but I'd like to banish it right now. I researched the scientific literature and explored numerous studies that have investigated negotiators' offer patterns and outcomes. In none of those investigations did it harm negotiators to open first. In fact, negotiators who make the first offer uniformly do better than those who don't. One caveat: In the rare and undesirable situation in which the other party knows more about you than you know about him, it is a disadvantage to open first.

Why do negotiators who make the first offer do better? Your opening offer acts as a powerful psychological anchor in a negotiation. It carries a lot of weight. Your opening represents the most you can (usually) hope to get. Don't underestimate how important opening offers are. Indeed, negotiators' first offers can generally predict the outcome of a negotiation. Adam Galinsky and Tomas Mussweiler found that first offers correlate as much as 85 percent of the time with outcomes.[6]

Many negotiators live in fear of the winner's curse, believing that the counterparty will gleefully and immediately accept their first offer. Don't come to the silly conclusion that you can make outrageous offers and expect to do well. Unfortunately, offers wildly outside the zone of possible agreement (ZOPA) lose their anchoring power and lead to a chilling effect, where a negotiator grows cold on a deal because he feels that the other party is not bargaining in good faith, or even the boomerang effect, which occurs when a ridiculous offer invites

> Many negotiators live in fear of the winner's curse, believing that the counterparty will gleefully and immediately accept their first offer.

an equally ridiculous counteroffer, often as a matter of spite. For these reasons, your ideal offer should be close to the other party's barely acceptable terms.

No one is going to accept your first offer, so making a concession is inevitable.

Strategically speaking, your aspiration point should be slightly worse (for the other party) than your guess about the other party's BATNA. The logic: No one is going to accept your first offer, so making a concession is inevitable. If you open with an offer that matches the other party's barely acceptable terms, you'll never end up there. It's best, then, to open with a figure slightly worse than the counterparty's barely acceptable terms. If your opening offer is dramatically worse, you create a chilling effect. If it is just a tiny bit worse, you are in the domain of the counterparty's acceptability range. Offers in this range are, by definition, not insulting.

TRUTH

16

What if the other party makes the first offer?

Once you know that scientific evidence supports the negotiator who makes the first offer, you may go so far as to cover your ears when you realize that the other party is about to present you with an opening offer.

But it's not wise to tune the other party out if she is ready to make you an offer. A better strategy is simply to remind yourself of your own first offer before the other party delivers hers. Preparing your opening offer is your best defense. Under typical conditions, however, most people haven't prepared their opening and are swept out to sea when the other party opens first.

Here are some handy points to think about in advance:

- If you haven't prepared an opening offer, you shouldn't be at the bargaining table. Remember, your opening offer is a behavioral manifestation of your aspiration point. So it's imperative to prepare your opening offer.

- If you state your opening offer like a demand, you instigate either the chilling effect or the boomerang effect. When your offer is insulting, the other party's motivation to reach a deal cools off (chilling effect). Outrageous offers might even invite retribution such that the other party is motivated to hurl back an insult (boomerang effect). However, you *can* make your offer in a nondemanding way. Here's how I do it in my personal negotiations:

"In the spirit of recognizing how important your time is, I have prepared a set of terms that would be acceptable to me. I understand, however, that you will most likely have some different ideas. So I offer this set of terms (which I have written on the flip chart over here) as a starting point for what I hope is a more broad-ranging discussion. And, in that spirit, I am eager to hear your ideas."

> If you haven't prepared an opening offer, you shouldn't be at the bargaining table.

Suppose that the other party has indeed beaten you to the punch and has made one heck of an opening offer. In that case, I would say, "Thanks for sharing your ideas with me. I've also

spent some time preparing
a set of terms that would
work for me. I will warn you
right now that my terms are

Always write down your opening offer.

dramatically different from the ones you've sketched. But, in
the spirit of recognizing the value of your time and beginning
our discussion, I'd like to share them with you. I am ready to
fully discuss all terms."

- Okay, you got flustered. Everyone does occasionally. So, here's
an idea: Always, I mean always, write down your opening offer.
If you find yourself tongue tied, you can always pull out your
notebook or turn your laptop around to share your ideas.
Anchors work dramatically better when you write them down.
So write down your opening offer on a flip chart or
blackboard. That way, you can continue to refer to it
during the discussion.

TRUTH

17

Plan your concessions

Few negotiations end after one round. Rather, there is a back and forth, with parties making offers and counteroffers. This is the dance of negotiation. I advise you to plot your offers and counteroffers with the precision that a football coach would bring to the Super Bowl. In other words, to prepare for an upcoming negotiation, you should know every stat about past negotiations: how many concessions you made, the size of your average concession, how many concessions the other party made, how far apart the two opening offers were, and so on.

> Plot your offers and counteroffers with the precision that a football coach would bring to the Super Bowl.

Why? Because people often get carried away by the momentum of the negotiation and fail to think analytically about the pattern of concessions. This leads to one or more of the following mistakes:

- You make concessions too quickly, before you explore interests.

- You make concessions that are too large. (In contrast, making small concessions creates goodwill and signals that you're reasonable but getting closer to your reservation price.)

- You make concessions while the other party remains intransigent.

To get in the habit of keeping track of the negotiation game, I strongly advise keeping a little notepad in front of you, even making visual sketches, rather than writing in paragraphs. That way, you can say things like;

> Look Pat, I want to point out that I've come down $50,000 since we started talking, and by my records, you've increased your offer by only $10,000 so far, or only one-fifth of what I've come down. (Such a statement puts pressure on the counterparty to make concessions.)

> Francis, I've made concessions on all the issues we're talking about; according to my records, you've only made concessions on one. I ask you now to consider what you could do on some of the other issues.

Sometimes, negotiators make a plan they can't follow through on. For example, I've heard several negotiators plan to make no concessions. This is ill advised: If you refuse to make concessions, the negotiation quickly reaches a stalemate.

Sometimes, negotiators make the opposite mistake: They open with a great first offer, which is inevitably refused by the counterparty. On their next move, they make a too-deep concession, effectively giving up all their bargaining ground.

As a general principle, negotiators should make concessions on issues that are the least important to them. Don't expect the other side to give you credit for making a concession. They usually won't. For this reason, you need to announce your concession. Say something like,

> I've been listening to you carefully. My current offer on the issue of paid vacation days is 7 per year. I know you want that number to be higher. So, I have thought about it and I could live with 10 paid vacation days per year. (Get up and cross out 7 and write 10.) Thus, I'm willing to concede on this issue by increasing from 7 to 10 days.

Note that in the preceding statement, the negotiator is doing four things: (1) reminding the counterparty of an opening offer of seven days; (2) drawing attention to the fact of being willing to make a concession on that issue; (3) writing the new number on the board, another way to create quid pro quo pressure; and (4) explicitly inviting the other party to respond.

If you don't invite the counterparty to respond, he has much less incentive to make a concession.

If the counterparty doesn't write down the numbers proposed, take over the board yourself.

I would advise you as the negotiator in this scenario not to make further concessions on any of the issues until the counterparty has made a concession. When making concessions, if the counterparty doesn't write down the numbers proposed, take over the board yourself. I've seen too many negotiations break down because of "miscommunication." Words and proposals fly back and forth, but everyone gets confused when it comes to actually writing the exact terms.

Suppose the counterparty does indeed make a concession. At this point, you might want to make another concession—again on an issue that is less important to you. I advise negotiators to reduce the size of their concessions with each successive offer, to signal to the counterparty that they are nearing their reservation point.

TRUTH

18

Be aware of the "even-split" ploy

The following interchange actually occurred. What, if anything, is wrong with this picture?

Party A: I'll offer you $15M to buy your company.

Party B: Are you kidding? It's worth much more than that, and I have several offers. I would want at least $47M.

Party A: That's a lot more than I'd ever want to spend. The most I could offer would be $18M.

Party B: Well, then we probably won't reach a deal, because the company is worth $47M. But I might agree to $46M.

Party A: Still unacceptable. My highest bid would be $22M. But that would have to be with a closing in the next 30 days.

Party B: I don't think I could accept that offer. I'm not trying to drive a hard bargain, but I think we both realize this company is special. I would agree to $45M.

Party A: My final offer is $25M.

Party B: Okay, I have an idea. Why don't we just split the difference, for an even $35M? That would be fair to both of us.

Party A: That sounds fair, I guess.

Upon first glance, three things jump out about this negotiation.

First, the party's opening offers of $15M and $47M are wildly apart. There is a divide of $32M. That's not atypical.

> It's almost inevitable that one negotiator will suggest "splitting the difference."

Second, both parties make concessions in a somewhat quid pro quo fashion. That's advisable, per the previous Truth. However, I would encourage Party A to invite another concession from Party B because Party A made three concessions, while Party B made two concessions.

However, the real problem for Party A is not the *number* of concessions she made, but the *magnitude* of those concessions. Party A made concessions of a depth of $10M (initial offer of $15M, and most recent offer of $25M). In contrast, Party B made concessions one-fifth of that depth, or $2M (initial starting offer of $47M and most recent offer of $45M). Party A will probably never recover from this blunder.

It's almost inevitable that one negotiator will suggest "splitting the difference" to close the gap. The emotional appeal of this ploy is overwhelming for most fair-minded negotiators, to the point that it seems selfish and egotistical to refuse. The problem in the previous negotiation is that Party A made much deeper concessions than Party B. Yet when Party B suggests splitting the difference, it's as if the past never occurred.

> In our rush to wrap up negotiations and show good faith, we often make concessions that are too steep and quick.

This is why I strongly caution negotiators to carefully plan their concessions. In our rush to wrap up negotiations and show good faith, we often make concessions that are too steep and quick.

TRUTH

19

Reveal your interests

Many negotiators have been advised to not reveal any information to the other party. However, failure to reveal information about interests can lead to lose–lose agreements, as in the case of the "Orange Sisters," who failed to discover the win–win solution. The trick is to know what type of information to reveal. As a general rule, hide your BATNA but reveal your interests. Just how big is the impact of revealing information on a negotiator's bottom line? Negotiators who provide information to the other party about their interests improve their outcomes, or profits, by over 10 percent.[7]

So, why is there so much reluctance among negotiators to reveal information? There are a few reasons. First, conventional negotiation wisdom holds that negotiators should maintain poker faces at all times. It is unfortunate that well-meaning colleagues and mentors have coached so many negotiators to conceal everything. This advice has led to a shrinking of the pie of resources under negotiation. Second, most people constrain their definitions of "information that could be revealed" to BATNA-related information rather than anything about their broader interests.

> Negotiators who provide information to the other party about their interests improve their outcomes, or profits, by over 10 percent.

Negotiators can reveal, or "signal," their interests in several ways. Direct disclosure is one method; subtle signaling is another. All of the following statements can significantly expand the pie. Consider adding them to your negotiation vocabulary:

- "Issue X is more important to me than Y, but I care about both."

- "A 10 percent gain on issue X would be more valuable to me than a 10 percent gain on Y."

- "If I were to rank order the issues' importance, X would be higher than Y."

Also consider adding the following questions to your negotiation vocabulary:

- "Which is more important to you: X or Y?"

- "What would give you more value: increasing X or increasing Y?"

- "If I were to increase payment on X but decrease payment on Y, would that be better for you?"

> A major benefit of revealing your interests is that you double the probability that the other party will disclose hers.

A major benefit of revealing your interests is that you double the probability that the other party will disclose hers. This mirroring reflects the *reciprocity principle*. For example, in one of my investigations, I found that under normal conditions, the incidence of providing information to the other party was 19 percent. But when negotiators provided information to the other party, it jumped to 40 percent, based on the reciprocity principle.[8] Keep in mind, however, that reciprocity also applies to antagonistic behavior.

TRUTH

20

Negotiate issues simultaneously, not sequentially

Many people negotiate in the same way that they run their business meetings: by strict agenda. They simply list all issues under negotiation and then attempt to reach an agreement on each one, in sequence. Unfortunately, negotiating each issue independently is not only exhausting, it increases the likelihood of lose–lose agreements. Why? Negotiators are more likely to adopt a demanding, positional approach on each issue; they fight each battle and lose perspective about what is ultimately the most important issue. A far better approach is to discuss issues as packages and combine issues.

The key for negotiators is to handle several parts of a deal at the same time. This approach has several advantages. First, it prevents negotiators from being completely positional. Second, it forces them to prioritize their values and preferences across several issues. Third, it may spark the brilliant idea of considering packages or combinations of agreement terms.

> **The key for negotiators is to handle several parts of a deal at the same time.**

Consider a case of two negotiators discussing three issues in a sales deal: price, volume, and delivery. Ms. Buyer wants a low price, low volume, and fast delivery. Mr. Seller wants a high price, high volume, and slow delivery. On the surface, their interests seem completely opposed. In other words, it looks like a fixed-sum negotiation.

Now imagine that Ms. Buyer has carefully laid out the priority she gives each issue by splitting 100 points among them: 50 points for price, 35 for delivery, and 15 for volume (see the following buyer table).

As the seller table reveals, Mr. Seller's values for the three negotiation issues are a little different: Price is also his most important issue (50 points), but volume is second (35 points) and delivery last (15 points).

We also see that Ms. Buyer ideally wants lowest price, lowest volume, and fastest delivery. If that happened, based on the table, she would get $20 + 5 + 15 = 40$ points. That represents the buyer's desired objective.

BUYER	Price (50 total)	Volume (15 total)	Delivery speed (35 total)
Low (slow)	20	5	0
Med-low	15	4	2
Med	10	3	6
Med-high	5	2	12
High (fast)	0	1	15
SELLER	Price (50 total)	Volume (35 total)	Delivery speed (15 total)
Low (slow)	0	0	5
Med-low	5	2	4
Med	10	6	3
Med-high	15	12	2
High (fast)	20	15	1

Let's suppose these parties decide to negotiate each issue separately. Remember that in the real world, they wouldn't know each other's preferences. Here's how the negotiation might go:

Buyer: It has been a real pleasure to learn about your product. But I have to be honest with you: We are price restricted. We absolutely need your lowest price.

Seller: Well, we have a great-quality, unique product. So we deserve a high price.

Buyer: Then we might not have a deal.

(One hour passes.)

Buyer: We seem to be at two extremes on price. How about we just meet in the middle?

Seller: I guess we can live with that.

Buyer: Okay, then let's talk about volume. We want to minimize our commitment here, so we need only a small lot of your product.

Seller: Unfortunately, we're designed to sell big lots. But you'll definitely love our product, so you're better off with a bigger volume, anyway.

Buyer: I'm not authorized to approve that.

83

Seller: Well, the price we talked about is based on a high-volume purchase.

(Another hour passes.)

Seller: There is no way I can go with that volume. I might be able to meet you in the middle, though.

Buyer: That would work.

Seller: Let's talk about delivery. We can offer our standard terms.

Buyer: No, we need this ASAP!

Seller: Sorry. Our policy clearly states that our standard delivery is several weeks.

Buyer: That just won't work. I'm being way too generous, but can we meet in the middle again?

Seller: I'll probably lose my job, but in the spirit of closing this deal…okay.

The buyer and seller would each make a total of 19 points on this deal (buyer gets the sum of medium price = 10; medium volume = 3; medium delivery = 6; and seller gets 10+6+3).

Had they negotiated the issues as a package, they might have realized that volume was relatively more important to Mr. Seller, whereas delivery speed was more important for Ms. Buyer.

That could have led to the following conversation:

Buyer: I see several moving parts to this deal: price, volume, and delivery. We care about all these issues, but price is most important. And we need to get to market fast, so we also care a lot about delivery.

Seller: We need a reasonable price, so I definitely can't concede too much on price. But my company cares a lot about volume, so we can give better prices with bigger lots. We might be able to work with you on delivery.

Buyer: Would you be willing to give me the fast delivery I need if I buy a greater volume?

21

Logrolling
(I scratch your back,
you scratch mine)

Logrolling is making mutually beneficial trade-offs between the issues on the table.

The term *logrolling* is derived from political science, where it describes how one party might support another's bill or legislation in return for reciprocal support. In that domain, logrolling has a slightly sleazy connotation. In negotiation, logrolling is smart, not sleazy.

To logroll effectively, negotiators must do the following:

■ Identify more than one issue under negotiation. (Otherwise, there is no possibility for trade-offs.)

■ Have different preferences concerning the issues.

■ Be able to mix and match different alternatives for each issue.

If a negotiator is positional or demanding, logrolling will be much more difficult. Logrolling is the art and science of being firm but flexible. A negotiator needs to be firm about the issues most important to her but flexible on things that are not as important. For example, consider Veronica, a busy executive who was "negotiating" with a childcare provider (babysitter). Hourly wage was hugely important to the babysitter, but for Veronica, having control over the provider's vacations was the most important issue. The solution? Higher pay in exchange for vacation timing controlled by the employer!

> A negotiator needs to be firm about the issues most important to her but flexible on things that are not as important.

It's hard to imagine why negotiators fail to logroll when it would clearly be in their best interests. The key roadblock is the destructive and pervasive fixed-pie perception. Negotiators may erroneously assume that the other party's interests are directly and completely opposed to their own interests. In this sense, they falsely project their unique preferences onto the other party.

It is far more likely that the other party will have preferences and values different from ours. This asymmetry gives negotiations much more potential for win–win outcomes.

Consider how the buyer and seller in the previous truth could logroll:

> *Buyer*: It seems that there are three issues under consideration: price, volume, and delivery. Do you see it that way? I care about all the issues, but frankly price is most important, delivery is a close second, and I have some flexibility on volume, but only if I can get good terms on the other issues.

> *Seller*: Thanks for sharing that. My company cares about price, so we can't be too flexible there. But I'm interested in your ideas on volume and delivery. We are a volume-based seller. So, I need to be firm on volume, but I can often meet just-in-time delivery needs, provided that you can meet our price and volume needs.

> *Buyer*: That gives me an idea. What's more attractive to you: medium volume and medium delivery or high volume and fast delivery? We'd rather go with high volume and fast delivery.

> *Seller*: My company is in complete agreement on that. So should we go with the highest volume and the fastest delivery?

> *Buyer*: That's what I am saying.

Secretly, you and I know that Ms. Buyer and Mr. Seller each net 16 points on this volume–delivery trade-off. Further, agreeing on a medium price would give them each 10 points. That results in 26 points for each party. This is a dramatic improvement over the 19 points they got in the no-tradeoff agreement. One of them might even get a promotion. Beyond that, both of them have gotten closer to their target and, most importantly, there is no alternate deal that is simultaneously better for both parties.

TRUTH

22

Make multiple offers of equivalent value simultaneously

One negotiation strategy that virtually guarantees that negotiators do not leave money on the table is the multiple-offer strategy. How does it work? First, before beginning the negotiation, the negotiator has to unbundle the issues.

For example, consider the story of Evelyn. When seeking a job, she took the advice of a savvy employment counselor, and when her interviews led to a discussion about her salary history, she avoided the topic, saying instead, "Let's see if we're a good fit for each other before we talk about that issue."

The interview went well, and the decision maker was clearly interested and began the negotiation for what Evelyn's total remuneration package might be.

Obviously, salary was important to Evelyn, but given that she was a single mother, there were several other key factors: work hours flexibility, ability to do private consulting in the office space in the evenings (Evelyn is a therapist), reimbursement for clinician training and testing (to become licensed), and, of course, number of paid vacation days per year. Thus, Evelyn was able to identify five issues: salary, flextime, consulting privileges, licensing fee reimbursement, and vacation days.

As a second step, Evelyn knew she had to prioritize the issues. That was hard. So she pictured 100 poker chips in her mind and stacked them up in five piles to reflect how important each of the five concerns was in relation to the others. This is how she eventually stacked up the chips:

Salary (50)

Consulting privileges (20), a lucrative way to enhance her income

Flextime (15)

Licensing fee reimbursement (5)

Vacation days (10)

Evelyn was like most other people: Salary was very important to her. But, as you see, other issues could make or break her quality of life. In particular, having some flexibility in her schedule and having the ability to use the office for her private consulting practice were important concerns.

After unbundling and considering the priority of the issues, the next step for Evelyn was to create three combinations of relatively equal value to her: packages A, B, and C:

Evelyn was like most other people: Salary was very important to her. But other issues could make or break her quality of life.

Package A: Salary of $100,000 (what the company was offering), complete flextime, three weeks of paid vacation, reimbursement for licensing fees, and unlimited consulting.

Package B: Salary of $130,000, no flextime, three weeks of paid vacation, no licensing fee reimbursement, and consulting opportunities under control of the employer.

Package C: Salary of $120,000, three days a week of flextime, no licensing reimbursement, consulting opportunities for two days a week, and three weeks of paid vacation.

Evelyn looked hard at these until she was certain she felt indifferent about which of the three packages she was offered. She was at the point where she would be willing to roll the dice and have the employer choose any of these, and she would feel equally happy.

TRUTH

23

Postsettlement settlements

"Who's your favorite negotiator?" people often ask me. Many expect me to say Henry Kissinger or Donald Trump. But instead I say Professor Howard Raiffa of Harvard University. Wait, you might say, aren't professors just armchair theoreticians? Howard Raiffa is a gifted theoretician, to be sure, but he is also an amazing negotiator. And his book *The Art and Science of Negotiation* is chock-full of brilliant approaches to real-life negotiations.

When I first read Raiffa's description of postsettlement settlements, I was struck by its utter simplicity and elegance. Yet I haven't met a single business person who knew about it. Once they learn about it, though, they become like me: addicted.

So, what is a postsettlement settlement?

Bob and Susan Sanderson are fitness fanatics, but they draw the line when it comes to hauling massive specimens of new exercise equipment to their home and down the stairs to their home gym. So, when they responded to a sale at their local Costco by buying an unbelievably heavy new contraption for their home, they negotiated with Costco to have it delivered to their home. Those were the terms.

The day of the arrival came, and the driver was visibly not happy to have to heft the great and clumsy box from his truck into their house. As a matter of fact, he stated that he would only deliver to the front steps. Not *up* the steps, just *to* the steps. Ideally, the Sandersons wanted him to come through the garage and down the stairs into the basement. No doing.

The Sandersons took this as an opportunity to create a postsettlement settlement. They correctly ascertained the delivery driver's interest to be primarily financial and theirs to be primarily physical—meaning Bob did not want to have hernia operation #3. So, the Sandersons suggested that perhaps for an additional $50, the delivery driver might be willing to bring the contraption through the garage and down the stairs to the gym. They also determined that one of his concerns would be to avoid them accusing him of soiling their carpet or damaging their house. They said that they were not worried about the carpet and would take responsibility for any damage if the thing slipped. They also iced the cake by mentioning that they would pay in cash.

Thus, a postsettlement settlement represents a mutual improvement over a given deal that both parties currently find acceptable.

About 75 percent of negotiators, given an opportunity for a postsettlement settlement, are able to mutually improve upon the deal.

A postsettlement settlement represents a mutual improvement over a given deal that both parties currently find acceptable.

Think also about the motivation that negotiators have when they go back to negotiate after a deal has been reached. If they think they can bully, badger, or harangue the other party into giving up more of the pie, they would be sadly mistaken. Rather, negotiators must realize that the only way to improve their own outcomes is by improving the other party's outcomes.

TRUTH

24

Contingent
agreements

If logrolling is a Chevy and a postsettlement settlement is a BMW, then a contingent agreement is a Ferrari.

Sometimes negotiators vehemently disagree about a current state of affairs or what can plausibly be expected to happen in the future. Sometimes such disagreements can be resolved by consulting experts or conducting research. However, negotiators often cannot resolve such disagreements because no relevant data exists, or negotiators disagree regarding the data's relevance or interpretation. In such situations, negotiators can reach resolutions by using contingent contracts.

Contingent contracts are if–then agreements that specify conditions under which specific actions will result in specific outcomes. Smart negotiators use contingent contracts in many, if not most, business negotiations. They do this because contingent contracts open up the possibility of win–win deals; they capitalize on negotiators' differing views of the world.

> Contingent contracts are if–then agreements that specify conditions under which specific actions will result in specific outcomes.

Picture this scenario: The state of California was surprised by an earthquake. Okay, it wasn't surprised, but it hadn't planned on an earthquake right then. The Nimitz Bridge had collapsed, preventing the crossing of San Francisco Bay. Bridges were out and lanes knocked akimbo across that part of the state; in addition, sewage and drainage pipes were misaligned. The state needed help—and fast. It would get some federal money, but except by using a maze of makeshift detours, some hundreds of thousands of workers could not commute to work. So, what did the state do? Like any other government bureaucracy, the state shifted into high gear and put out a call for bids to repair damages. This could take forever, right?

However, what the state did that is unusual, and pretty sharp, is that once the lowest bid was landed—and I won't go into how the system we favor means most things we drive on are built by the lowest bidder—it negotiated a delivery. The state knew that money was important to the contractors and that time was important to the state's getting back to normal.

The contractor knew the reality of how long it takes to build or repair roads on this scale. But it also had an eye on its bottom line: Show me the money!

So the state negotiated a contingency contract for the delivery of the sum of all repairs needed. It set an aggressive deadline: six months. If the contractor delivered all the repairs on time, it would get a multimillion-dollar bonus. This put both negotiators on the same side of the table. The state wanted the repairs done quickly, and the contractor wanted as much money as it could get.

What they eventually landed on was an agreement with the stated bonus and also penalties if the contractor went over the agreed-upon deadline. The contractor was willing to shoulder the risk of making less money in the face of the opportunity to make much more. And, don't you know, all those repairs were made on time, well within the deadline. The contractor got its bonus, and traffic was back to normal in the state of California.

Think about a negotiation in which your view of the world was misaligned with the other party's. Could you have crafted a contingent agreement?

Think now about a time when you had a different risk attitude than your counterparty did. Perhaps you were risk averse and the counterparty was risk tolerant. Might you have crafted a contingent arrangement based on this mismatch? There was one instance in which my husband and I disagreed about whether I would be able to drive back to our house from an appointment in time for him to drive my car to an important event. (For various reasons, we both wanted to use my car.) Because he was much more risk averse than I was in this case, I told him that if I failed to return by a certain time, I would buy and prepare all the food for the dinner party we were hosting the next week, a task we normally would have shared. He took me up on the proposal (which, by the way, I lost).

Another case in which contingent agreements may be used is when negotiators have different time preferences. Some people want immediate payoffs; the counterparty might be more interested in long-term payoffs.

To be effective, contingent agreements should meet three criteria, at minimum: incentive alignment, enforceability, and measurability. First and foremost, continent contracts should not give negotiators an incentive to work at cross-purposes to each other. Rather, contingent contracts should align objectives, as in the case of the California road repair construction. Second, I strongly encourage negotiators to formalize contingent contracts in writing, with appropriate legal counsel. Finally, but still importantly, decide in advance how the terms of the agreement will be measured.

> To be effective, contingent agreements should meet three criteria, at minimum: incentive alignment, enforceability, and measurability.

PART 4
PSYCHOLOGY

It helps to know about human psychology when seated at the bargaining table. If you are unaware of these key principles, you may be vulnerable to common negotiation ploys.

TRUTH

25

The reciprocity principle

Shortly after the United States entered World War II, the Americans joined the British in launching costly bombing raids over Germany. Part of the intent was to demoralize the Germans and break their will. The US and UK believed that a series of steady bombing raids would demoralize the Germans and cause them to retreat. However, the plan to demoralize did not work. Research reports conducted by the Office of Strategic Services that compared heavily and lightly bombed areas did not find significant differences in civilians' will to resist.

Several other conflicts have followed the same psychological pattern—for example, Pearl Harbor, South Africa, and North Vietnam. In all of these instances, the aggressor works under the faulty belief that aggression will lead to submission in the target. However, inevitably, aggression invites aggression.

The reciprocity principle is probably the most important but least understood concept in psychology. It characterizes relationships among people, groups, and warring nations. The reciprocity principle is quite simply the tendency for people to treat others the way they are treated.

> The reciprocity principle is quite simply the tendency for people to treat others the way they are treated.

Salespeople understand the reciprocity effect. Excellent salespeople know that small acts of generosity create powerful psychological obligations that result in big sales. For example, a real estate agent might treat you to a latte during an open house showing, which might obligate you to buy a house from one of their listings. Certainly the price of a latte pales in comparison to earning a 6 percent commission on a $225,000 house. But, too often we forget scale in our haste to reciprocate favors. So, be wary about accepting favors and if you do, think about size.

The reciprocity effect does not know cultural boundaries, as it has been documented in nearly every country in the world. And feelings of indebtedness to others run deep: If one group receives a favor from another group but is unable to return the favor immediately, it carries that debt into the next generation to repay.

Why, then, do so many well-meaning negotiators behave like bulldogs in negotiation and wonder why the other party chooses to escalate instead of back down? The answer, I think, is simple: We hold a psychological double standard when it comes to using force. We think that if we use force, we can intimidate and weaken the other party. Yet we believe that if someone uses force with us, we will retaliate. Assume that the counterparty is every bit as smart and motivated as you are.

So, when you think about flexing muscle in a negotiation, be warned that doing so will most definitely increase the probability that the counterparty will flex his muscle, too.

> Assume that the counterparty is every bit as smart and motivated as you are.

If the reciprocity principle characterizes the use of aggression and competition in negotiation, it certainly applies to the cooperative, constructive aspect of negotiation. In other words, if I use a trusting, relationship-building strategy in negotiation, have I increased or decreased the probability that you will respond in a constructive, trusting fashion? Answer: I have increased it.

TRUTH

26

The reinforcement principle

A group of sneaky students got together before class and decided to test the power of the reinforcement principle. Whenever the instructor walked on the right side of the classroom, they attentively smiled, nodded, and sat forward in their seats. However, when the instructor paced over to the left side of the classroom, the students slumped, averted their eyes, and disengaged. On which side of the classroom did the teacher spend the most time: the right or the left? The obvious answer is that he spent dramatically more time on the right side of the classroom. The students had positively reinforced the speaker's behavior. Yet, the instructor was unaware of why he ended up on the right side of the room by the end of the lecture. This brings up an important point about reinforcement: It occurs at a level below our threshold of awareness.

Under what conditions would you want to use reinforcement in negotiation? Answer: Anytime you want to increase a certain behavior. In negotiation, people emit various behaviors, some pleasant and constructive, and some offensive and destructive. Ideally, we want to encourage the counterparty to emit behaviors that will help us expand the pie. We can do this if we follow certain principles of behavioral reinforcement.

> Under what conditions would you want to use reinforcement in negotiation? Answer: Anytime you want to increase a certain behavior.

As simple as this psychology sounds, it is easy to screw it up. The main things to remember about reinforcement are these:

- **Be immediate**—We're talking about seconds when it comes to rewarding behavior. If you wait several minutes to nod and smile to the counterparty, you have missed your window to reward her behavior.

- **Be unambiguous**—Your reward should be clear and simple, such as a clear and simple nod, an open smile, eye contact, or a heartfelt compliment.

- **Reward behaviors, not underlying states**—The reinforcement principle works great when it comes to behaviors. Don't get caught up in trying to reward an attitude, a disposition, or an intention of the other party. My rule of thumb is to stick to whatever behaviors can be pointed to. For example, don't try to reinforce someone for speaking truthfully. However, reward someone for opening up his binder or sharing a company report.

- **Be consistent**—If you sometimes reward a given behavior and sometimes fail to acknowledge or even perhaps punish that same behavior, you send a mixed message to the other party. Be consistent in your rewards.

All of the following actions may be considered rewards in most contexts. They build a cooperative foundation and do not require us to make concessions:

- Smiling
- Nodding
- Maintaining eye contact (in many cultures, but eye contact in some cultures can be threatening and a sign of dominance, not liking)
- Verbal phrases such as "I like that," or "I appreciate that," or "That is great," or even "Tell me more."

TRUTH

27

The similarity principle

Think about the last social event you attended where you met someone for the first time. Chances are, you spent the first part of your conversation trying to establish a point of similarity. When people meet for the first time, they relentlessly search for a point of similarity. For example, "Do I detect a Texas accent?" "Have you ever met my friend Rhonda?" "Where did you go to school?"

The irrepressible urge to find a point of similarity in others is hardwired in most of us. It is our primitive way of sizing up whether someone is friend or foe, threat or opportunity. Someone who is like us might share some of our gene pool and work with us, not against us.

Part of negotiation is trying to find a point of similarity. It is best to do this early on in a negotiation to help grease the wheels for agreement.

> The irrepressible urge to find a point of similarity in others is hardwired in most of us.

Evidence for the similarity principle is overwhelming. In one investigation, people were randomly divided into two groups: dot overestimators and dot underestimators. (Everyone had to guess how many dots were on a page.)[9] Then each person was informed that he or she was either a dot overestimator or a dot underestimator. (Of course, they were actually told at random if they were dot overestimators or dot underestimators.) Next, they engaged in negotiation with someone who was either described as a dot underestimator or a dot overestimator. The results were dramatic: People behaved much more cooperatively with people who were part of the same dot estimator group. This was shocking because who in the heck cares about dots anyway? The point, however, is worth noting: People cooperate more with others who are supposedly similar to them and compete more with others who are different from them. It certainly behooves all of us to find a point of similarity with the counterparty.

In another investigation, marchers in a political demonstration were more likely to sign a petition if the requester was dressed like them.[10] Moreover, they signed the petition without even reading it when the requester was dressed similarly to them!

The similarity principle works also for social networks. If you can find a common point of connection that is a similar person, this creates a psychological obligation to like the other person. Suppose, for example, that Mary is negotiating with Ned. They have never met, but Mary learns that Ned knows (and likes) Jose. Mary also likes Jose. This means that Mary and Ned are most likely going to want to get along, to put the entire social network in a state of harmony.

It certainly behooves all of us to find a point of similarity with the counterparty.

28

The anchoring principle

In one investigation, people were asked to guess how many African countries are in the United Nations.[11] Most people don't know the answer to this question without doing a Google search, so they guess. In this particular study, people were standing in front of a wheel of fortune. Half of the time, the researcher spun the wheel of fortune, and it landed on a high number (such as 100); the other half of the time, the number was much lower (such as 10). How did the random wheel-of-fortune number affect people's judgments about the number of African countries in the United Nations? Even though it is illogical for a random number to have anything to do with making this guess, it strongly affected people's judgments. The people who saw the high number adjusted their guess downward, but not downward enough. (The average guess was 50.) The people who saw the low number adjusted their guess upward, but not upward enough. (The average guess was 15.) The actual number of African countries in the United Nations is 53.[12]

What is interesting about the wheel-of-fortune study is that everybody knows that wheels of fortune are based on chance. Thus, in some sense, people should have completely discounted the number that was displayed on the wheel of fortune. This brings up another important point about the anchoring effect: Even when the initial anchor is obviously arbitrary or downright silly, it still exerts a powerful impact on people's judgments.

People tend to make judgments based upon an initial starting point and then adjust upward or downward, but they fail to make sufficiently large adjustments.

The anchoring effect refers to the fact that people tend to make judgments based upon an initial starting point and then adjust upward or downward, but they fail to make sufficiently large adjustments.

Another example: People were asked to guess how many physicians were listed in the Manhattan phone book. Certainly, no one knows that information off the top of her head. Some people were first asked whether the number was greater than or less than 100. Other people were first asked whether the number was greater than or less than 1,000,000. Obviously, there are more than 100 doctors in Manhattan, but certainly there aren't as many as a million. However, these two different anchors caused people to make very different guestimates about the number of physicians in Manhattan.

In negotiation, your opening offer acts as an anchor—and so does the counterparty's opening offer. This means that a counterparty's outrageous opening offer may psychologically anchor your own perceptions about what you can attain in the negotiation. I have seen several negotiators get "pulled out to sea" when the other party drops an aggressive opening anchor. The solution? Determine your opening proposal before hearing the counterparty's opening.

> Anchors have more staying power when they are supplemented with facts, data, and logic.

Anchors can be numbers, but they can also be your supporting arguments and data. Anchors have more staying power when they are supplemented with facts, data, and logic. Thus, it is much more powerful to justify your opening offer with relevant information and facts than to simply state the offer.

29

The framing principle

Which would you rather have?

A. $10,000 for sure

or

B. A 50–50 chance of winning $20,000 or nothing

This tantalizing proposition is an approach–approach conflict because both options are pretty attractive. (We'd like both of them!) However, we have a little bit of an internal conflict in choosing because as much as we would like to get $20,000, there is a 50 percent chance that we would walk away with nothing. When most people are given the A or B choice, the large majority choose A. (About 85 percent of the students in my MBA and executive courses would rather have $10,000 for sure than a 50–50 chance of winning twice as much money.)

This phenomenon illustrates a basic tenet of human behavior called risk aversion. When it comes to choosing among attractive courses of action, most people would rather have a bird in the hand than go beating around the bush.

However, let's turn the tables around. Imagine that someone has you at gunpoint in a dark alley, late at night, and offers you the following choice:

> When it comes to choosing among attractive courses of action, most people would rather have a bird in the hand than go beating around the bush.

C.   Lose $10,000

or

D.   Submit to a 50–50 chance of losing $20,000 or nothing

(To make this seem more real, imagine that this person has the ability to extract this money from you.)

This is an avoidance–avoidance conflict because neither option is attractive. In fact, both options suck. However, you are being held at gunpoint, and you have to choose. The majority of people in this situation choose the gamble—in other words, they opt to flip the coin and take a risk that they might lose a huge sum of money, but they might not end up losing anything. This behavior illustrates a basic tenet of human behavior called risk-seeking behavior.

But now we have a conundrum: How can people be both risk averse and risk seeking?

This is where Nobel Prize–winning psychologist Daniel Kahneman of Princeton University comes to the rescue. According to Amos Tversky and Daniel Kahneman, whether people avoid or embrace risk depends upon how the problem or decision is framed.[13] When people are asked to make approach–approach decisions (that is, choosing a sure good thing or a gamble that might lead to something much more attractive), most people are risk averse. However, if that same problem is framed as an avoidance–avoidance problem, the tables turn and people are much more likely to gamble!

Indeed, almost any decision in our lives can be framed as a gain or a loss relative to something. Quite frankly, our point of reference for defining gains and losses is pretty arbitrary. A reference point defines what a person considers to be a gain or a loss. Savvy negotiators know how to frame the offers they make to the other party by carefully selecting points of reference.

> Indeed, almost any decision in our lives can be framed as a gain or a loss relative to something.

Max Bazerman, Tom Magliozzi, and Margaret Neale demonstrated the powerful framing effecting negotiation. They told some negotiators that they should try to "cut their losses"; they told other negotiators that they should try to "maximize their gains."[14] However, in both cases, their objective financial situations were completely identical. In other words, the only difference was how the negotiators framed their own financial situation.

Bazerman, Magliozzi, and Neale expected that the negotiators who were told to cut their losses would behave a lot like the person confronted in the dark alley: In other words, they would behave in a much more risk-seeking fashion. That is what happened: Negotiators who were put the mindset of cutting their losses made fewer concessions in the negotiation and reached more impasses than did negotiators who were told to maximize their gains. In short, these negotiators took a gamble by refusing all offers in hand and decided on a risky course of action that involved walking away from a sure deal (in hopes of a better deal!).

This effect clearly shows that negotiators who have the mindset of minimizing their losses adopt more risky bargaining strategies, preferring to hold out for a better but more risky settlement. In contrast, negotiators who are told to maximize their gains are more likely to take the bird in the hand.

Obviously, it is in your best interest to put your opponent in a "gain" frame. This will increase the chance that the opponent will take your offer. If the counterparty views your proposal as a loss, he will do something risky, like stalking out of the room.

The framing effect is a powerful, two-edged sword: You can frame others, but you can also be framed! So, before any negotiation, think about your reference points!

PART 5
PEOPLE PROBLEMS (AND SOLUTIONS)

You prepared. You planned your opening. You are committed to win–win negotiation. But you did not get the memo that you would be negotiating with Mr. or Ms. Psycho. So, now what?

30

Responding to temper tantrums

Several negotiators, such as Donald Trump, are renowned for throwing temper tantrums at the bargaining table. Often this means hurling china plates, stalking out, making threats, and using verbal abuse. Is this behavior effective in eliciting concessions from the counterparty?

In a staged study simulation to determine whether it is a good or bad idea to display negative emotion at the bargaining table, negotiators were given a "deteriorating best alternative to a negotiated agreement (BATNA)," meaning that their alternative courses of action were disappearing fast, and the only game that was left in town was to work with Negotiator X.[15] Negotiator X was coached to adopt one of three emotional styles: very cordial and considerate (Ms. Nice), extremely rude and demanding (Ms. Temper), or neither rude nor nice (Ms. Neutral). All the negotiators were then put in a take-it-or-leave-it situation by Negotiator X. The question was which of the three emotional styles would be most effective. It turns out that Ms. Temper was the least effective. Perhaps out of spite or perhaps because they were so angry, no one wanted to give business to Ms. Temper, even when their BATNAs were rapidly deteriorating.

In another investigation, a negotiator made a take-it-or-leave-it offer and in some conditions, made a joke (for example, "I will throw in my pet frog"); the other half of the time, the negotiator did not make a joke.[16] In both these situations, the contents of the offer were the same. However, acceptance rates were not the same. People liked the negotiator with the sense of humor more than the humorless negotiator.

Many temper tantrums are not genuine. Rather, they are carefully orchestrated displays of emotion designed to evoke a response in the counterparty. This is the difference between felt emotion and strategic displays of emotion.

Many temper tantrums are…carefully orchestrated displays of emotion designed to evoke a response in the counterparty.

So, what to do? If someone—perhaps even yourself—is throwing a temper tantrum, whether staged or authentic, I suggest using one of more of the following strategies.

First and foremost, take a break. Sometimes people just need a few minutes to reflect and collect themselves. Also, it is a good idea to take a break if you feel you are about to say something you might regret.

Second, normalize emotions. You can do this by saying something like, "This is a significant matter for both of us. It is normal to feel emotional about something this serious...."

Finally, stop talking and start writing—preferably on a flip chart or white board or smart screen. Writing serves several purposes: It is known to be therapeutic; people who are writing are more likely to reflect. It is far more likely that someone might shout "You are a jerk" than to write "You are a jerk" on a whiteboard. Writing creates a point of focus. Finally, when negotiators are stuck, they can summarize points rather than battle about what has been said.

TRUTH

31

How to negotiate with someone you hate

You will almost certainly have to negotiate with some people who have pathological personalities. You need to figure out a way to deal with the mental cases you have to negotiate with. Medicating the other person is not an option, so what can you do?

There are three important things to keep in mind when it comes to dealing with difficult people at the negotiation table:

- Replace "D" (dispositional) statements with "B" (behavioral) statements.

- Label your feelings, not people.

- Change your behaviors, not your feelings.

Let's take each of these points in turn because if you become consumed by feelings of hate and repulsion for the other party, you are not going to be able to negotiate effectively.

Replace D statements with B statements

Consider the following statements, actually made by negotiators:

"Jack is impossible to deal with."

"Larry is always a jerk when we sit down for budget meeting."

"My supplier, Elizabeth, is psychotic in sales negotiations."

These are all examples of type D statements because they focus on the counterparty's dispositions. Type D statements (or dispositional statements) are characterized by the belief that a given person behaves the way she does because of her personality or disposition. A dead giveaway for a type D statement is the word *always* (for example, "Elizabeth *always* does such and such," "Jack is *always* this way.") Type D statements locate the root of the cause of a person's behavior to that person's fundamental disposition rather than think of it as a reaction to a situation he might be in. Type D statements are character assassinations.

> If you become consumed by feelings of hate and repulsion for the other party, you are not going to be able to negotiate effectively.

What is the solution? Replace type D (disposition) statements with type B (behavior) statements. All of the following are type B statements:

"I hate the fact that Jack is consistently late to meetings."

"I don't like the way Larry treats the junior people on the team."

"I resent it when Elizabeth changes her mind after committing to a deal."

Parents often fall into the trap of making type D statements with their kids: "You are annoying," "You are acting like a baby," or the worst, "You are bad." The parents should rephrase these statements like so:

"The way you are playing that music is annoying me."

"Being asked the same question by you for the past 30 minutes makes me feel short-tempered."

"Breaking DVDs is not acceptable in this house."

Label your feelings, not people

When you make statements like "You are acting crazy," "She is aggressive," or "She is making me lose my temper," you are relinquishing all responsibility to the other party for your behavior.

Take more ownership for your negative relationships by taking more responsibility for your own feelings. Even if you can't change your feelings, you can take more responsibility. Consider the table that follows. On the left side are common statements people make in the heat of argument. On the right side are reformulations in which negotiators take more personal responsibility.

Typical statements made that do not take personal responsibility	Reformulations of these statements that reflect ownership and responsibility
"You are making me mad."	"I am feeling short-tempered."
"She is too aggressive."	"I feel resentful when I am given ultimatums."
"You are screwing up the deal."	"I feel that it is unwise for me to make a deal."
"Your offer is ridiculous."	"I am disappointed with the progress we are making."

Change your behavior, not your feelings

You most likely have a few "complex relationships" in your negotiation life—relationships that are necessary for you to engage in but cause you anxiety for a variety of reasons. You may have tried unsuccessfully to change your feelings about the counterparty—perhaps engaged in endless amounts of self-talk or made personal pledges to try to change your feelings about a person—yet nothing works. You still harbor resentment toward this person.

It is perfectly okay to have venomous feelings for another person. Don't try to change those feelings, at least right now. Instead, commit to changing your behavior. Be proactive. Think of three acts of cooperation you are going to commit to with the "complex relationship" in the next 10 days. Here are some steps you can take to get rolling:

- Stop by this person's office just to say hello.

- Send this person's subordinate a nice email, complimenting her on a job well done.

- If appropriate, give this person's superior a compliment about her.

- Invite this person to lunch without business intent.

- Send this person a book or DVD that you know would be welcome.

You can even take responsibility one step further: The next time you are interacting with Ms. Complex Relationship, raise the issue of how you would like to improve your working relationship. Ask if she might share the same goal. Most often, the other person sees you as the complex relationship. Suggest some ideas. Ask for feedback. Shake hands.

TRUTH

32

How to negotiate with someone you love

Negotiating with someone you love, deeply respect, or have had a long-term relationship with is not always the walk in the park you might think it should be. Husbands and wives and dating couples are quite likely to settle upon lose–lose outcomes!

When we think about negotiations with people we love, there is a past, a present, and a future. When there is a lot at stake, emotions can run high. So it is best if you have a working approach.

Most of the negotiations we do in our personal lives with people that we love arise when we experience conflict. Conflict occurs when people perceive themselves to have incompatible interests involving scarce resources (for example, who gets the family car for the evening), goals (for example, where to go on a family vacation), or procedures (for example, how to discipline children).

Many of the business negotiations we've discussed in this book have focused on purely transactional (buyer–seller) relationships. The parties in those situations sought one another out because they saw an opportunity to make a trade. For example, a seller and buyer might see a mutual opportunity. Opportunity moves people to negotiate. However, people in long-term relationships are not brought together by business opportunity; instead, they step on each other's toes and need to resolve conflict.

When it comes to conflict in personal relationships, your own view of what is going on in the relationship may not be at all what your partner thinks. Sometimes, conflict may not exist, but people feel that it does; other times, people are not aware that they have a conflict. Consider this table:

	Actual conflict	No actual conflict
Perceived conflict	Real conflict	False conflict
No perceived conflict	Latent conflict	Harmony

Note that when conflict actually exists and people perceive it, that is real conflict. When there is no actual conflict but people believe there is, that is a case of false conflict. Conversely, when conflict exists but people fail to perceive it, that is latent conflict.

Harmony speaks for itself!

Once you determine whether conflict is real, you need to decide what your reaction to it is going to be. According to psychologist Carol Rusbult and colleagues, there are four possible reactions: exit, loyalty, neglect, and voice.[17]

Exit occurs when one person leaves the relationship to seek greener pastures. When you exit a relationship, you actively exercise your BATNA.

Loyalty means you stay with your partner and just tolerate him. It means that you accept his terms and capitulate. You might simply accept the first thing he suggests and never assert your own aspirations. People are often afraid that they will hurt or insult the other party, so they capitulate to the other party. We are often uncomfortable negotiating with people we love. This, of course, is the ultimate form of capitulating. People put their own interests on hold in personal relationships because they put a greater value or utility on resolving conflict than they do on the actual outcomes involved. When people do this over time, they may rationalize, or they may become resentful.

Neglect is a passive strategy for dealing with conflict. It occurs when parties are in a standoff or at an impasse. Neither a standoff nor an impasse is a real discussion, and neither is seeking greener pastures. Unfortunately, this holding pattern will certainly cause the relationship to deteriorate.

Voice occurs when people proactively try to talk about the conflict and make things better. Voice is an active strategy. It quite literally means that both parties articulate their concerns and views on the conflict. When it comes to voice, don't underestimate the power of letting people vent and express themselves. Here are some of my favorite techniques for initiating a proactive discussion:

> When conflict actually exists and people perceive it, that is *real* conflict. When there is no actual conflict but people believe there is, that is a case of *false* conflict. When conflict exists but people fail to perceive it, that is *latent* conflict.

- "I need to talk to you about something that is bothering me. I want to try to work things out before I start feeling resentful."

- "I feel uncomfortable talking about our finances (or car, travel schedules, household chores), but I am unhappy with our current situation and suspect you feel the same."

- "The recent change in our finances (or travel schedules, work commitments, and so on) has led to some unanticipated and undesirable effects on me. I have some ideas to talk to you about how to make it better."

TRUTH

33

Of men, women, and pie-slicing

What is the difference between men and women when they negotiate?"

You may consider this, as I do, a loaded question. So, let's look at a few research-based facts:

- When men and women negotiate against one another, such as in a buyer–seller arrangement, men get a larger slice of the pie. This statement is not based on old data; salary discrepancies between men and women are growing, not shrinking. In 2003, the wage gap between men and women graduating from elite MBA programs was almost negligible. However, by 2013, the pay gap had significantly widened. Female grads earn 93 cents for every $1 earned by their male classmates.[18] Sound like chump change? Think again. Suppose a man and a woman are both offered a $50K salary at the outset of their career. Suppose the man negotiates a 10 percent increase, but the woman does not. Now, assume that both get a steady 5 percent annual raise every year. The man will earn over $600,000 more over a 40-year career than his female colleague.[19]

- Men are more likely to initiate negotiation (for example, attempt to negotiate their job offers and salaries) than are women. Why? For one thing, women believe that assertive behavior will elicit a negative response. Depressingly, they have every reason to be on their guard: Women who "ask" are not viewed as positively as men who ask, and evaluators "penalize" women who ask for more.[20]

- Women set lower aspirations or targets than do men, all else being equal (that is, holding constant their previous experience, education, etc.).

Okay, we've got a problem. So, how to fix it? In my own research on this thorny subject, my colleagues Laura Kray, Adam Galinsky, and I wondered whether the typical stereotype of women being docile, nice, and nurturing might actually be hurting them. Indeed, we found that when women (and men) were reminded of the archetypal female stereotype of being accepting, nurturing, kind, and submissive, women claimed much less of the bargaining pie. [21]

We obviously needed to try to turn around this situation. We found that two scenarios—mindsets—can really help women at the table. Let's call the first mindset the *backfire effect*. In one of our scientific tests, we decided to be up front about the typical female stereotype. Rather than be politically correct and not say it or speak it, we clearly referenced the female stereotype as one in which females are accepting, giving, empathic, and so on. (We were banking on the fact that the high-powered females in our management and executive courses would think that this was a bunch of baloney.) They apparently did. They ended up claiming more of the pie than men did, and they claimed more of the pie than when we made absolutely no mention of the classic female stereotype. Thus, in some sense, if there is a gorilla in the room, it helps women to say that there is a gorilla in the room.

Several years ago, Professor Howard Raiffa compiled a list of 38 characteristics of successful negotiators in his book *The Art and Science of Negotiation*. As it turns out, some of those 38 characteristics are male sounding (for example, assertive, dominant), some are traditional female sounding (for example, empathic, good at nonverbal skills), and some have no gender connotations (for example, punctual). When my colleagues and I gave a mixed group of negotiators a redacted version of Professor Raiffa's list featuring the female-sounding "effective negotiator characteristics," the women in the group did much better than when they were given the male-redacted list or a neutral list. Everybody did the same negotiation. Despite the fact that everyone had the same objective financial situation and the same reservation price, the mindset we had created exerted a profound influence on how well the females in the group did. Let's call this the *right brain mindset*, because the right side of the brain is the part of the brain that is skilled in language, nonverbal behavior, and so on.

> In some sense, if there is a gorilla in the room, it helps women to say that there is a gorilla in the room.

The point is not that men are taking advantage of women or treating them tougher than they would treat males. But, rather, as Louis Pasteur once said, "Chance favors the prepared mind." Females who prepare their own mindsets should fare better in negotiation than those who don't.

34

Your reputation

Think about your past 10 negotiations. How many were one-shot negotiations, in which you did not expect to see this person or his company ever again? How many were long-term or repeated negotiations, in which you would probably see this person or his company in the future?

Chances are, fewer than 10 percent of your negotiations are truly one shot. Therefore, you need to think about and protect your reputation in most negotiations.

Think of your reputation as your social capital at the negotiation table. Your reputation is composed of three different things: (1) the personal brand or image you project; (2) people's firsthand dealing with you; and (3) secondhand information about you (gossip).

> Chances are, fewer than 10 percent of your negotiations are truly one shot. Therefore, you need to think about and protect your reputation in most negotiations.

In one investigation of the reputations earned by students in a negotiation class, the students rated one another on the basis of firsthand experience. Four different kinds of reputations surfaced: [22]

- **Liar-manipulator**—someone who is willing to do anything to gain advantage.
- **Tough-but-honest**—This negotiator is known to be very tough, makes few concessions, but does not lie.
- **Nice and reasonable**—This negotiator is willing to make concessions.
- **Cream puff**—This negotiator will make concessions and be conciliatory, regardless of what the other party does.

Before reading further, what would be the reputation you would want to have in your own negotiation community? As it turns out, people treat you differently, depending upon your reputation. If you have a reputation of being manipulative, people act more competitively with you.

How we see ourselves is not necessarily how others see us. Take the case of deceptive behavior: Most negotiators believe that they are deceived on average 40 percent of the time. (Sometimes the rate is about 50 percent.) However, these same people admit to using deception in about 25 percent of their negotiations. Do these two statistics add up?

No, they don't add up. Why? I think there is one key reason: the double-standard effect. Quite simply, we evaluate others much more harshly than we look at ourselves. I am quick to believe that you misled me, but I rationalize my own behavior. It really does not matter how you look at yourself. You must consider your own reputation.

Be aware of the effects that result from the way you interact with the other parties during negotiation. The self-aggrandizing effect and gender effect may seem like obvious ones to avoid. But recall that the *way* you make statements has effects as well. When you point to the disposition of the other party, such statements give rise to two biases about other people: the halo effect and the forked-tail effect. The *halo effect* is the tendency to believe that if a person is smart, she is also kind. The halo effect is the tendency to believe that if a person is physically attractive, she is also witty. In short, a halo effect occurs when people generalize wildly on the basis of only one piece of good information. You can probably guess what the *forked-tail bias* is: If you are clumsy, I also am inclined to think you are unintelligent, and so on.

> Most negotiators believe that they are deceived on average 40 percent of the time. (Sometimes the rate is about 50 percent.) However, these same people admit to using deception in about 25 percent of their negotiations.

The way you approach and respect others, then, has a great deal to do with how they do the same to you, and that, in a nutshell, is your reputation.

TRUTH
35

Building trust

Trust in a negotiation is like lubricant in a car engine: Things go a lot more smoothly in its presence. Three types of trust operate in our relationships:

- Deterrence-based trust
- Knowledge-based trust
- Identification-based trust

Deterrence-based trust is based on the principle of carrots and sticks. If I want you to work for me, I might give you an incentive to complete a contracting job by offering you a bonus for finishing before schedule. (I offer you a carrot.) I might also have a penalty clause. (If you fail to finish the job by a certain date, I reduce the payment.) Deterrence-based trust is often based on contracts and monitoring. For example, if I hire you to work for me as a childcare provider, and I install a hidden video camera to monitor your behavior, this is a form of deterrence-based trust.

Deterrence-based trust is fairly expensive to use. (Think about the costs of the video camera and attorney's fees!) The other problem is that if you get wind that I am monitoring you, you might be upset. For example, the presence of signs reading "Do not write on these walls under any circumstances" actually increases incidences of vandalism as compared to signs that say "Please do not write on these walls" or having no sign at all![23]

For these reasons, many people in the business world use a different form of trust, known as knowledge-based trust. *Knowledge-based trust* is what is commonly referred to as a "gentleman's agreement" or "handshake understanding." Knowledge-based trust is trust that develops between people who have worked with each other long enough to feel that they know the other person and understand them and can predict their behavior. To be

> Knowledge-based agreements are not binding in a court of law, but they often have a binding effect on the people who make these agreements.

sure, knowledge-based agreements are not binding in a court of law, but they often have a binding effect on the people who make these agreements.

Most people prefer to work with people who are referred to them by a friend or colleague. Suppliers who regularly negotiate with certain customers are working on the basis of knowledge-based trust. For example, buyers and sellers post scores on Amazon.com, and freelancers and clients also score one another on freelancer.com. Interestingly, the diamond market in New York is based on knowledge-based trust. Knowledge-based trust is based on the fact that you and I are in a community in which we both have reputations and we both want to maintain our reputation.

Identification-based trust is based on the fact that we have aligned incentives. In identification-based trust systems, we have mutual empathy for each other.

If knowledge-based trust is based upon my knowledge of you, *identification-based trust* is based on the fact that we have aligned incentives. In identification-based trust systems, we have mutual empathy for each other. Identification-based trust means that other people have your value system—shared interests, values, and reactions to jointly experienced stimuli. For example, "You and I have the same high work ethic that comes from growing up where we did and putting ourselves through college." You should do your homework to find such commonalities and be sure to emphasize them. It is far easier to trust someone you feel is on the same page as you in life than to trust someone who is very different.

TRUTH

36

Repairing broken trust

Sometimes trust is broken in a relationship. How do you repair broken trust? Unfortunately, there is no sure-fire solution. Consider one of the following strategies.

Let them vent

People want to be heard. Letting people vent and blow off their steam does not mean you agree with them. It just means you are listening. So, let a

> You don't have to agree; you just have to listen.

person who feels wronged tell his side of the story. You don't have to agree; you just have to listen. Check to make sure you understand by summarizing what the other is saying. Ask the counterparty if you've got his side of the story straight.

Apologize

If you did something you regret, say so. If you failed to do something you wish you'd done, say so. Make sure the other person hears your apology loud and clear. One of the best ways to apologize is to do something symbolic. Send a colleague a bouquet of flowers or a hand-written note (as opposed to dashing off an email) or give her a bottle of her favorite wine with a note saying, "I'm sorry about what happened."

The problem is, many people think they don't have anything to apologize for. In other words, they don't feel they did anything wrong. In that case, apologize that there was a misunderstanding. I like all of the following sentences:

"I'm sorry that there has been so much confusion and anxiety around the issue of the new senior hire."

"I'm sorry you did not get the email that was sent."

"I'm sorry that this situation has caused you so much stress."

Focus on the future

Saying you are sorry is often an uncomfortable act. Resist the urge to revisit the past in excruciating detail. Instead, focus on the future. What can you do to make sure that this misunderstanding does not happen again?

Do a relationship checkup

Don't wait for misunderstanding to occur before you talk about how things are going. Do a relationship checkup before problems occur. Pop your head into this person's office and simply ask, "How are things going concerning [the product development/the budget allocations/the hiring of new staff]? Is there anything that I should be working on to make sure that I am following through with our discussion about this? It is important to me that we work smoothly and I don't disappoint you."

> Don't wait for misunderstanding to occur before you talk about how things are going.

Go overboard

Ironically, it is often when trust is breached that you get a once-in-a-lifetime opportunity to do something so wonderful for a person that he will never forget it. Let's say something happens that was not your fault but that shakes the trust in your professional relationship: Materials you sent arrived late and were ripped and smudged, unusable. You quickly send replacement materials, but you don't stop there. You include a personalized gift for everyone involved. Sure, it can cost, but the other party's trust is often restored, and your obvious over-the-top effort to make things right might even lead to more business that would not have occurred otherwise.

TRUTH

37

Saving face

According to negotiation expert Morton Deutsch, saving face is a negotiator's most sacred possession.[24] Face is the value we put on our public image, reputation, and status in negotiations.

Part of using power responsibly is creating a way that both parties can come back to the negotiation table without fear of social censure or loss of self-esteem.

Negotiators often get so caught up in who's-right and who's-wrong determinations that they make it virtually impossible for people to return to the table with their dignity intact.

> Face is the value we put on our public image, reputation, and status in negotiations.

Moreover, people in the United States often do not appreciate how important face-saving concerns are for members of different cultures. For example, if a manager challenges a colleague in the presence of their boss, this may be perfectly appropriate in Western cultures but may cause shame in cultures that are more hierarchical, where deference to authority is valued.

Saving face works in two ways: helping others protect and maintain their dignity and managing your own esteem needs.

All of us care about how other people see us, and we have our own need for self-respect. However, the following situations will heighten people's need to save face:

- When negotiations are conducted in a public setting
- When people are accountable to a group or a superior
- When people negotiate in teams (as opposed to negotiating as individuals)
- When there are status differences between negotiators
- When negotiators have naturally thin skin

You can measure negotiators' face-saving needs by using a scale, called the Face Threat Sensitivity (FTS) scale.[25] If you want to see how thin your own skin is, respond to these statements: 1. I don't respond well to direct criticism, 2. My feelings get hurt easily, 3. I am pretty thin-skinned.

People with high FTS scores have a lower threshold for detecting and responding to threats to their face (dignity). In other words, it does not take much to get them hot and bothered. Conversely, people with a low FTS have thicker skin; they don't see situations as making them look foolish, and they are not easily threatened.

In buyer–seller negotiations, fewer win–win agreements are reached when the seller has thin skin (high FTS). Moreover, in employment negotiations, job candidates with high FTS (thin skin) are less likely to make win–win deals.

> In buyer–seller negotiations, fewer win–win agreements are reached when the seller has thin skin.

Here are some of my favorite face-saving strategies to use if you sense that the other party has thin skin (and, therefore, a need to save face):

- Apologize for something. ("I don't like some of the things that came out of my mouth in our discussion today. I hope you can forgive me.")

- Compliment the person. ("I think your ideas about the pricing program are particularly ingenious and refreshing.")

- Say you care about the relationship. ("I know we are focusing on the business at hand, but I want to stop for one minute and do a relationship check and reiterate how important the relationship with you is to our company.")

- Talk about how you have learned important things as a result of this process.

- Ask for feedback about how things are going on the relationship ledger. ("Look, Steve, I am new in my role here, and I would love some of your feedback at this point in the process.")

- Point out the concessions you made. ("I am conceding to you on point X.")

- Focus on the future, not the past. (People are often preoccupied with justifying their past behavior.) One of my favorite lines from the book *Getting Disputes Resolved* is, "We are not going to agree about the past, but we might agree about the future."[26]

- If the other party says, "This is my final offer," don't respond with, "I don't believe you!" Instead, respond by saying, "I hear you, and I would like to respond to some particular points."

PART 6
I-NEGOTIATIONS AND
E-NEGOTIATIONS

The rise of information technology has led to new forms of negotiating. On the one hand, it is efficient; on the other hand, it creates new limitations. Like it or not, we behave differently when we are not face-to-face, and this affects the success of our negotiations.

TRUTH

38

Negotiating on the phone

Would you rather negotiate face to face or on the phone?

Proponents of face-to-face negotiation say that you get more information from several data feeds when you are face to face. These negotiators like the fact that they have access to a person's nonverbal as well as verbal behaviors.

Those who prefer the phone like the fact that they can use the phone as a buffer—to better compose their ideas and buy time.

Who is right? Actually, both are! If you are in a position of power, you are better off negotiating face-to-face because the other party is not able to counter-argue as effectively as you can. This can give you an edge when it comes to dividing the pie, or claiming value. However, if you have less power than the other party, opt for the phone so you can better manage when and how to respond to tactics.

When it comes to win–win agreements, there is a tendency for face-to-face negotiators to reach the most win–win outcomes, followed in success by telephone negotiators, and last, writing-only negotiators.[27]

Face-to-face interaction is the richest form of interaction because you have four channels of information feed:

- **Kinetic cues**—Kinetics means "touch," and in social interaction, touch is a way of establishing rapport. In negotiation, people establish rapport by shaking hands, high-fiving, pulling two chairs closer together, and so on.

> If you are in a position of power, you are better off negotiating face to face because the other party is not able to counter-argue as effectively as you can.

- **Visual cues**—Visual cues include anything you can see about the other party, such as whether she maintains eye contact, how she uses her hands, whether her body language is dominant or submissive, emotional expressions on her face, and so on.

- **Linguistic cues**—Linguistic cues refer to the actual content that negotiators use in their communication, such as the size of their offer.

- **Paralinguistic cues**—Paralinguistic cues refers to how a person uses language. For example, we can often detect sarcasm by the way a person emphasizes certain words.

When you negotiate on the phone, you lose the kinetic information feed, the sense of touching, and the visual information feed. This means you rely on linguistic cues and paralinguistic cues only. For this reason, people often have a harder time establishing rapport with the other person. Rapport is the feeling that you have when you are "in sync" or "on the same wavelength" with another person. Nonverbal behaviors, such as how you gesture and maintain eye contact and nod your head, are key to building rapport with someone. Have you ever had a phone call during which you and the other person were interrupting each other? This is a failure to synchronize.

> Rapport is the feeling that you have when you are "in sync" or "on the same wavelength" with another person.

When you communicate face to face with someone, you engage in a complex dance of verbal and nonverbal behaviors, in which you adjust your speech and bodies to ease social interaction. This social dance paves the way for more win–win agreements. In one investigation, some negotiators stood face to face, whereas others stood side by side (and, therefore, could not easily establish conversational rhythm based on bodily cues). The face-to-face negotiators reached deals more quickly and successfully averted a strike![28]

If you find yourself on the phone, rather than face to face, think about how to develop rapport with the counterparty. Here are some strategies that may pave the way toward smoother interaction:

- Engage in small talk or schmooze for the first five minutes, before getting down to action.

- Arrange for a short, face-to-face meeting before the phone call. (Having met someone face to face even one time can provide a foundation for rapport down the road.)

- Don't multitask when you are on the phone. (Shut off your email and don't call this person when you are simultaneously checking into your hotel.) If you are dividing your attention, you are unable to focus on the interaction, and you send a signal to the other party that she is not worth your time.

- One of the most problematic things about phone calls is turn-taking. Signal that you are finishing speaking your turn by saying something like, "Well, now that I have laid that out, I'm interested in your thoughts."

- End the phone call in a personal way. People tend to remember beginnings and endings, so close on a bright note.

TRUTH

39

Negotiating via email and the Internet

Mark Zuckerberg wishes he had not conducted a major negotiation via email with Paul Ceglia, an early investor in the Facebook startup, in 2003. In one of the email exchanges, Zuckerberg challenged the status of their agreement and suggested that they should enact a 50–50 partnership. Years later, Zuckerberg claimed that the emails were fake. However, you don't have to be a dot-com millionaire to enter into an e-negotiation that starts to unravel.

Flight attendant Billy Makedonsky was pleased with himself when he negotiated the purchase of the "perfect retirement home" for his 75-year-old mother with just a few mouse clicks. But it turned out the property was immersed in multiple bankruptcies, had been foreclosed in protested proceedings, and was shrouded by allegations of fraud. Had Billy been on site, he would have seen a 69-year-old squatter in the home, the former mayor of El Portal, Florida, who refused to leave the property without a long legal battle.[29]

When people negotiate via text or email, they lose one of the information feeds that provides insight into human behavior: They don't see that person or at least they don't see them at the time they are actually interacting. Our behavior changes when we interact via information technology. What do you need to know? Consider the following:

Get in touch with your inner nerd

In face-to-face interaction, often the most charismatic person with the good looks and commanding presence dominates the conversation. However, when people interact electronically, they can't see someone's muscular build, towering height, and charming good looks. Rather, their ideas have to carry the day. For example, email communication reduces status differences often found in groups. For this reason, it is often the case that STEM folks—science, technology, engineering, and math—have an advantage. Similarly, when groups of executives meet face to face, men are more than five times more likely to make the first decision proposal; however, when that same mixed-gender group meets via computer, women make the first proposal as often as men.[30] What does this mean? Prepare and don't be afraid to use data and facts that support your position. When a relationship is face to face, trust is based on emotional information, but when relationships are purely virtual, trust is based on cognitive abilities. When negotiating virtually, getting your facts in order will go a long way toward building trust.

Dr. Jekyll and Mr. Hyde

For the most part, when people interact face to face or on the phone, they often engage in the politeness ritual. They are generally pleasant to one another. However, in the absence of synchronous interaction, people unconsciously drift into a decidedly more aggressive, self-interested, and callous set of behaviors. For example, "flaming"—making incendiary comments and remarks—is eight times more likely to happen on email than in face-to-face interaction. In job performance reviews, appraisers give more harsh feedback when delivering it electronically than in person—even when they are evaluating the same "low performer." And, in email negotiations, people are more hostile than they are in face-to-face negotiations.

How can you make sure you don't become Mr. Hyde? Put a picture of the person you are talking to on your desk. Better yet, put a mirror on your desk. If you look up and see a scowl, this will act as a reminder to be pleasant and not drift into a dehumanized virtual orbit. In general, negotiations are more profitable when people are in a good mood and trust and like one another.

High rollers

In one telling investigation, managers were presented with a risky choice versus a sure choice. When the group was interacting face to face, they made less risky judgments than when the same group interacted virtually.[31] Why? In the absence of human cues, people become more risk tolerant, to the point of being reckless. This might have fairly serious implications for a negotiation in which there might be uncertainty.

For example, suppose that you have an opportunity to purchase an intriguing business property. In your excitement, you make a good-faith offer of $250,000 in your letter of intent to buy, conditional upon conducting a formal due diligence. However, during the formal due diligence process, you uncover new facts, including a pollution problem that requires expensive cleanup and a tax lien that has not been properly accrued. You still have an "out," given these problems, and so, the risk-averse course of action would be to either withdraw your offer or negotiate a lower price. The risky course of action would be to push ahead with the purchase of the property. When people make such decisions face to face, they are decidedly more cautious and risk averse.

First you see it, then you don't

Suppose you have a limited budget for travel, yet an engagement calls for protracted negotiations. Should you opt for a meeting early in the process or at the end—such as when things are winding up? If you have a limited budget for face time, get on the plane now and have a face-to-face meet and greet with the folks with whom you will negotiate. This early meeting will pave the way toward smooth relationships, even after you are out of sight. People in e-negotiations often feel compelled to get down to business too soon. So, take five minutes to engage in a non-business conversation.

When you do get to sit down face to face, put your cellphone out of sight. In fact, it is advisable to remove most of the technology from the room! Why? The mere presence of technology—such as a cellphone on a table—leads to worse interaction.[32]

Talk this way

People who dress like the boss and look like the boss are more successful. How do we leverage this on email and via the Internet? We rely on the power of words. Negotiators who show linguistic convergence—meaning they use similar or same words or phrases—are more successful than those who don't converge.[33] Moreover, using your opponents' language is time sensitive, meaning that negotiators who actively mimic their counterpart's language in the first 10 minutes of a negotiation get better outcomes, than those who mimic during the last 10 minutes—and this is true across cultures![34]

TRUTH

40

When negotiations shift from relational to highly transactional

One of my clients, Sam, came to me recently for advice. Sam is the CEO of a small, profitable company that makes highly specialized parts. His key customer is a very large company—which I will call Big Company. For over a decade, Sam had been the supplier for Big Company and enjoyed what he described as a highly personal relationship with the company's key representatives. Sam was stunned when his long-term customer announced that all future business contracts would be put up for online competitive bid. Sam learned that Big Company had its own website on which wanna-be suppliers would submit bids. Big Company essentially uses this site to get bidders to compete with one another on price. A bidding war occurs when there is one buyer (or seller) and there are multiple sellers (or buyers). For example: When Costco (a really big company) wants to find a source for wine, toys, or toilet paper suppliers, it sets up competition among the wanna-be suppliers to lower their prices—often dramatically—in the hopes of being the supplier of choice.

Sam is not alone. Several of my clients—even large ones—have had the unsettling experience of customers and clients attempting to commoditize their products or services. A commodity is a good or service where there are no special, distinguishing characteristics among individual units of the good or service. Big negotiation deals, like Sam's, or negotiations such as selling a company or choosing a supplier for all of Europe are normally done in one of two ways: negotiating exclusively with one or only a few bidders (like Sam was used to doing in a face-to-face context) or by running an auction and inviting as many interested parties as possible to bid competitively. Nothing makes suppliers more furious and scared than their products being commoditized because then it becomes what I call a bleeding war: Whichever supplier can slash prices to the lowest level will gain the business. And, then, this same process is repeated again when the contract—often very short—expires.

So, is there anything that Sam's company can do once Sam realizes he is being dragged into a bidding war? There are six key things to keep in mind.

First and foremost: Know your best alternative to a negotiated agreement (BATNA) and don't agree to anything less than your bottom line. By technical definition, you should be willing to walk away from the table rather than accept something that is worse than your BATNA. Often times, I see my clients fall into "BATNA drift": They lose sight of the BATNA and get pulled into the current situation. Practically, this means negotiators should stop rationalizing. I have worked with several clients who have "taken one for the team," which is another way of saying that they reached a really poor deal in the hope that their sacrifice would be remembered and rewarded at some later point in time. This would make sense if it were in writing, but it is only in the heads of the rationalizing wanna-bes. Unfortunately, big companies don't have such memories, and even if they did, they are not there to pay it back.

Second, if at all possible, submit bids that are not single issue. By definition, negotiations that involve only a single issue—such as price—are purely win–lose or zero-sum games. There is no possibility for win–win.

Third, make multiple bids with different price points that come with different terms and conditions. By submitting multiple price points and connecting them to particular services and features of your product, you implicitly signal how your product is *not* simply a commodity. Even more importantly, the likelihood of discovering a win–win value-added trade-off increases exponentially.

Fourth, if possible, ask for feedback on initial multi-item bids and then study the feedback and use the insights to fashion a revised bid. If possible, find out whether there is a real-time conversation stream available; if not, suggest it. Indeed, when conversation and social-emotional components are included in e-commerce negotiations, negotiations go more smoothly.

Fifth, find out what the company's switching costs are. Big companies often threaten to drop current suppliers unless the current supplier matches or beats what happens to be the most recent competitor's ridiculously low price—and this creates the bleeding war. However, switching is not easy. Rather, it is often a threat that big companies don't want to face. How do we know this? Consider what happened to Brady, a senior leader at a major big data analytics firm. Brady was bitterly disappointed when a key healthcare customer chose to go with a lower-cost provider. However, in less than six months, the customer came back, after realizing the hard way that its data management problems were not being solved…and in fact were being exacerbated by the low-cost provider. The competitor's data analysis did not provide for the nuances unique to the customer's organization. Brady's only regret is failing to realize his key point of differentiation earlier!

Finally, don't panic. Contrary to popular wisdom that auctions mean that sellers get better prices, an exhaustive analysis of 400 companies sold by either auction or classic negotiation reveals that the sale prices were largely the same.[35] Why? Well, some companies just don't put themselves out there, fearing that they may overpay or sell out. And, as noted, face-to-face negotiations often bring in more issues and create more win–win deals. Bottom line: Even big companies should consider engaging in face-to-face negotiations.

TRUTH

41

Negotiating across generations

The Boomer stood aghast as he watched his Gen Y, 20-something colleague show up at the long-awaited, multi-million-dollar business negotiation wearing jeans and a t-shirt with the words "honey badger" emblazoned on it. The Boomer prepared for the meeting and brought out a lined parchment paper notebook, ready to share ideas. The Gen-Y kid was absorbed with his iPhone. Needless to say, the meeting was a disaster.

Negotiations between members of different generations can be more profoundly confusing than negotiations between people who don't share a common language. Unfortunately, there is no Rosetta Stone—at least yet—that tells us how to deal with such generational differences. What do negotiators need to know? And, how much are you willing to adjust?

By the way, before you think that you don't have to worry about prepping for negotiations with Gen Z—people born in 1997 or later—think again. Hannah Altman of West Bloomfield, Michigan, started her company, Hannah's Cool World, at the tender age of 9 in 2010. Hannah is more than in her comfort zone using information technology, whether she is communicating with her customers in the United States, Canada, and the UK or designing her website.

For all practical purposes, there a five generations: Matures, Boomers, Gen X, Gen Y, and Gen Z. Most generations are known for key events—or flashbulb moments—that shaped their understanding of the world, how they deal with people, and their value systems.

Matures, born sometime before 1946 and also known as Traditionals, experienced World War I and World War II as flashbulb moments. Their early experiences involve sacrifice and putting aside immediate self-interest. Their negotiation values include personal sacrifice, compromise, and making steady progress. Their spoken word is sacred for them.

Boomers, born between 1946 and 1964, also known as the "Me" generation, put their focus on personal achievement and mastery of their life course. One of their flashbulb moments was Neil Armstrong and Buzz Aldrin walking on the moon. Their negotiation values are nothing short of win–win. The handshake is sacred for them. In their worldview, nothing is impossible and everything is negotiable.

Generation X, born between 1965 and 1985, is also known as the "Latchkey" generation because they came of age as their Boomer parents self-actualized by pursuing educational and job fulfillment. Meanwhile, Gen X'ers got used to third parties—daycare, nannies, and fast food. Also known as the "MTV" generation, Gen X saw the rise and fall of the cold war and the onslaught of mass media. Their negotiation values are highly transactional and often involve looking at what is immediate, as opposed to the long term.

Generation Y, born between 1981 and 1997, also known as the "First Digitals" or the "Echo Boom," experienced the Persian Gulf War and the rise of the Internet. They watched young, edgy hipsters become millionaires overnight with their dot-com ideas. However, they did not grow up with iPads in hand and days spent on the Internet. To Gen Y, the hard work of the Boomers and putting in time and education do not matter as much as having 15 minutes of fame. Generation Y negotiators value speed and are used to having to adapt to change. When they negotiate, they are less interested in your facial expressions than they are in your apps.

Generation Z, those born after 1997, also known as the Millennials or the "I" generation, grew up watching the fall of the World Trade Center, the crash of the financial markets, and the intoxicating greed of financial moguls. They are not just comfortable using information technology, they often prefer it over face-to-face interaction. They are a generation that prides itself on multitasking. In negotiation contexts, they use their power by posting rather than confronting. Their networks are key. In fact, you can learn more about a Gen Z'er by reading her Facebook page than through a face-to-face interview.

Okay, so now you know what to expect. The question is: Are you willing to adapt and modify your behavior? Before you say, "Well yes, but I don't know where to begin…" consider the following steps:

1. Hire a generational coach. Okay, that is probably not an actual job title, but find someone in your office of the era in question and quiz them: What are your biggest pet peeves about your generation? How do you show respect? Disrespect? What is the most interesting thing you have read? Watched?

2. Spend a day with your coach. Go to his chosen restaurant, watch his shows, and find out what he does for entertainment.

3. If you have time, set up a mock negotiation and go overboard with it—each of you acting like a caricature of yourself. If you can deal with extremes and stereotypes, you will probably fare much better in the actual throes of intergenerational negotiation.

174

TRUTH

42

Negotiating
with different
organizational cultures

In a widely publicized TV ad campaign, a stuffy, bloated Bill Gates look-alike patronizingly chides an extremely cool and relaxed hipster who looks reminiscently like Steve Jobs. The cultures of the two iconic companies—Microsoft and Apple—are about as compatible as oil and water. It's a case of Mr. Suit meeting Mr. Blue Jeans. Corporate cultures can be so distinctly different that they cause friction between otherwise well-meaning negotiators.

Just as every human has a unique personality, every organization has its own culture—a system of shared values about what is important and beliefs about how things work that shape norms and expectations of how people should behave. According to Bruce Tharp, company cultures vary in terms of two key values: how flexible they are and whether they are internally versus externally focused.[36] This creates four possible types:

- **Compete culture (stability and external focus)**—Microsoft is an example of a compete culture. Players in compete cultures are driven by market worth and economics. The negotiators from these cultures conduct careful due diligence and focus on what the market offers. They are highly rational and use economics to make decisions. They behave and think in a self-interested manner, and they assume that others are self-interested as well.

- **Collaborate culture (flexibility and internal focus)**—Some companies treat their employees like family. For example, the Perkins Coie law firm is routinely heralded as one of the best places to work. Partners in the firm treat one another like family and close friends. The firm is highly flexible in terms of adjusting to meet the needs of the employees, and the focus is on excellence.

- **Create culture (flexibility and external focus)**—Apple is an example of a create culture. Sometimes known as adhocracies, create cultures value experimentation and exploration. For example, the company Evernote Software offers its employees unlimited paid vacations because it believes doing so stimulates creativity.

- **Control culture (stability and internal focus)**—Many governments and schools are examples of control cultures. These corporate cultures are based on strict hierarchies, and reporting relationships are clear.

These are some best practices to keep in mind when negotiating between different organizational cultures:

- Be aware of how others perceive your organizational culture. In short, be aware of whatever stereotypes might exist about your company or industry. True, they are most likely incorrect or exaggerated, but unfortunately, your negotiation counterparty holds this perception as well.

- If the stereotype is negative, don't try to deny the view that your counterparty has about your industry or company, but instead describe your own approach to the business negotiation. It is very hard to change stereotypes; on the other hand, it is much easier for people to make exceptions to stereotypes. So, be willing to be viewed as the exception. Of course, if the stereotype of your company is positive, then leverage that!

> It is very hard to change stereotypes; on the other hand, it is much easier for people to make exceptions to stereotypes.

- Find out the corporate culture of the person with whom you will negotiate. Does the person come from a control, create, collaborate, or compete culture? If that person is from a compete culture and you are from a collaborate culture, be forewarned!

TRUTH

43

Negotiating with different demographic cultures

Cultural differences can dramatically affect negotiations. For example, when people from the United States and people from China were shown a picture of a group of swimming goldfish and asked to make a one-sentence summation of what was going on, the stories the people from the two cultures told were diametrically different.[37] Americans told stories of leadership and taking the helm. Stories about CEOs and their direct reports were not uncommon. People from China told stories about community members attempting to catch and protect a teammate and stories about the importance of working in the community.

The U.S. stories were about leadership and individual effort. The Chinese stories were about community and team effort. These different stories illustrate one of the most profound differences among cultures: individualism versus collectivism.

Individualists see the world as their oyster. They see themselves as independent entities acting upon the world. They don't accept circumstances. They fight for what they want.

Collectivists see the world as a big tapestry, in which they represent one thread that makes a whole pattern. Collectivists take others into account when making decisions. They are willing to make adjustments so that the community can be best served.

Individualists and collectivists also give themselves away with their pronouns. Individualists use many more *I*, *me*, and *mine* pronouns; collectivists use many more *we*, *us*, and *our* pronouns.

Cultural differences can also lead an unsuspecting negotiator into a barbed-wired fence.

One young woman from the United States, Elisa, shared a depressing story about a cross-cultural negotiation in her company. At age 26, she was an engineer responsible for product development. Her team, which happened to consist of three men and herself, counted on her as their "knowledge leader."

Her trip to Asia was a complete failure, however. It was not because she failed to prepare. From the first moment of making contact with the counterparty, she was treated as a secretary. She was expected to take notes, make tea, and pick up supplies. The counterparty directed all conversation to the men on her team and did not acknowledge her. She was not invited to several key meetings—even though she was the lead negotiator.

My student had walked unsuspectingly into a hierarchical culture. Hierarchical cultures are traditional cultures that recognize males, tenure, seniority, and rank. Hierarchical cultures are based largely on who has status in society. Elisa lacked gray hair, and she had the wrong chromosomes. It did not matter that her team saw her as the lead negotiator; the counterparty did not acknowledge her. The senior people in hierarchical cultures are to be respected, and it is their job to take care of those who are dependent upon them.

> The next time you negotiate with someone from a different culture, take the time to find out how that person views the world.

Elisa, of course, had been a member of egalitarian status systems all her life. In egalitarian cultures, the merit of one's ideas determines one's status in an organization. In egalitarian status systems, there are status layers, but they are permeable through hard work and smarts.

The next time you negotiate with someone from a different culture, take the time to find out how that person views the world. Don't assume that your view of the fish swimming is his story.

PART 7
NEGOTIATION YOGA

Negotiation, like yoga, is a journey. You will never arrive at a final end state. The key is awareness.

44

What's your sign? (Know your disputing style)

Which of the following phrases have you used or heard used in a negotiation? Be honest. Better yet, ask your colleagues how they see you. Give yourself 1 point for each phrase you have ever said and 2 points if you say something like it often. If a particular phrase is not in your vocabulary, give yourself a 0.

1. ____ That's not the way we do things here.

2. ____ That is my final offer.

3. ____ You will have to do better than that; otherwise, we don't have a deal.

4. ____ What is your most important issue?

5. ____ According to my records, that is not what we agreed to.

6. ____ I want to share some of my interests with you.

7. ____ I am calling my attorney (or any mention of an attorney).

8. ____ That is the most ridiculous thing I have ever heard.

9. ____ I would like to understand more about your key value drivers.

Add up your Power score—that is, your scores on items 2, 3, and 8. Next, add up your Rights score—your scores on items 1, 5, and 7. Finally, add up your Interests score—your scores on items 4, 6, and 9.

* * *

Jeanne Brett spent several years in coal mines, watching extremely contentious negotiations between labor and management unfold. She did the same thing at airline negotiations with union reps and management. In her book *Getting Disputes Resolved* (with coauthors Steve Goldberg and William Ury), she discovered that nearly everything that people said could be chunked into one of three major buckets: interests, rights, or power. Accordingly, Brett, Ury and Goldberg developed their theory of disputing styles called the Interests, Rights, and Power Model (or I–R–P Model):[38]

- **Power**—Power moves are any statements that attempt to force another person to do something he would otherwise not do. Parents do this with children, and people of different status levels do this a lot. For example, "If you don't do X, I will terminate you." Power moves also include one-upsmanship and hurling insults. Threats to withdraw business are power moves.

For example, one sister might say, "If you don't give the orange to me, I am going to tell mom that you drove her car without asking."

- **Rights**—Rights moves are moves that reference standards, norms, customs, rules, guidelines, legal rights, or precedents. Statements such as "This is not the way we do things" and excessive focus or bureaucracy are examples of rights-based moves. A rights-based negotiator attempts to invoke precedents. A rights-based sister might say, "I sent you an email dated February 22, 2013, in which I claimed that orange."

- **Interests**—Interests-based negotiators attempt to get past the demands that the parties might have and focus on the underlying goals and interests. An interests-based sister might say, "What are your most pressing interests regarding the orange? For me personally, I need to get my scone business going, so having that zest is imperative."

If your Power score is highest, you tend to use power moves in your negotiations. If your Rights score is highest, you use rights-based moves. If your Interests score is highest, congratulations—you use interests-based negotiation, which is usually most effective.

Once you know the I–R–P Model, it is impossible not to spontaneously categorize people. For example, the other day, I witnessed a blue car make a sharp lefthand turn to grab a coveted parking spot. The blue car pulled quickly in front of a white car that was poised to turn right into the same coveted space. The driver of the white car immediately shot the finger (power move). The driver of the blue car explained that he indeed had his blinker on before the other car did and therefore was entitled to the space (rights-based move).

The same thing happens in airports. Think about a scene at a ticket counter, where an angry customer is demanding a ticket change. The gate agent refuses. The angry customer demands to see her boss (power move). The ticket agent recites rules printed on the back of the ticket (rights move). The even angrier customer says, "Hey, I can read. I went to school" (power move). The ticket agent then says, "Sir, you will have to leave; I have to serve other customers" (rights move). Finally, the superior emerges and says, "What is the problem here? Let's take a look at what we can do" (interests-based move).

The point here is not that you need to always use interests-based phrases and extinguish rights- and power-based phrases from your vocabulary. Negotiators need to be trilingual. You need to be able to use interests, rights, and power at the appropriate times.

> Negotiators need to be trilingual. You need to be able to use interests, rights, and power at the appropriate times.

Satisficing versus optimizing

Reaching true win–win agreements is not easy. More often than not, from an objective perspective, you can spot a deal that both parties would like more—often dramatically more—than the one they agreed to. This means that both parties settled for less than they should have.

Consider once again the fateful story of the sisters negotiating a single orange. One of the sisters wanted to drink all the juice from the orange, while the other wanted the whole peel to make scones. Instead of being clear about what they wanted, they both made the same demand: "I want the orange." They finally split the orange in half. One sister drank the juice from her half and threw out the peel; the other sister used the peel from her half and discarded the juice. Managers and executives often reach outcomes tantamount to cutting oranges in half. They are oblivious to the existence of another feasible agreement that would have been far more beneficial, just as the sisters would have been much better off by splitting the orange into juice and peel!

This brings us to a key question: Why do people settle so willingly for lose–lose agreements? There are three main reasons:

- Satisficing
- Lack of feedback
- The fixed-pie perception

Satisficing

Nobel Laureate Herb Simon coined the term *satisficing* for the human tendency to suboptimize—to work just enough to achieve a mediocre goal. Simon contrasted satsificing with a much more productive behavior: optimizing.

First and foremost, negotiators just plain set their sights too low.

One early satisficing experiment asked people to multiply $1 \times 2 \times 3 \times 4 \times 5 \times 6 \times 7 \times 8$.[39] Most people tackled this by multiplying the first few numbers and then making an educated guess at the answer. However, on average, their answers were way too low.

A different group was given the same numbers to multiply, but in reverse order: $8 \times 7 \times 6 \times 5 \times 4 \times 3 \times 2 \times 1$. This group made better guesses, but their answers were still totally wrong. The results indicate that people rely excessively on mental shortcuts and take "cognitive naps" that can result in costly mistakes. In other words, people are lazy.

Another study compared the negotiations between spouses and dating couples to those between strangers.[40] It seems reasonable to guess that married and dating couples, presumably interested in nurturing a long-term relationship, would reach the most win–win outcomes. They didn't. Complete strangers had a greater incidence of win–win outcomes than couples! Why? Satisficing. On average, the couples quickly settled for the first set of tolerable terms. In contrast, the strangers were more inclined to think about their ultimate aspirations and explore more routes to achieving these. This optimizing led to more win–win agreements.

> People rely excessively on mental shortcuts and take "cognitive naps" that can result in costly mistakes.

Lack of feedback

A second reason people fail to reach win–win deals is that they simply don't get feedback about their agreements. Thus, most people have no objective idea about the outcome of their negotiation. As a result, their behavior becomes self-reinforcing. This is akin to someone eating highly fatty foods, never exercising, never checking her blood pressure, and proudly concluding, "I'm not dead, so I must be healthy." This person is operating without knowledge of her actual health and, more importantly, what she could do to maximize it.

I strongly encourage everyone to seek opportunities to put their negotiation skills to the test—by seeking feedback.

The fixed-pie perception

A third reason for lose–lose agreements is related to the "fixed-pie perception," or the nearly universal belief that one's own interests are diametrically opposed to those of the other party.[41] It epitomizes the win–lose type of thinking that marks most negotiations. If I believe that you are wholly opposed to whatever I want, we don't have much opportunity to create a win–win deal.

You will encounter an alarmingly high incidence of fixed-pie perceptions since many people falsely believe that the other party has preferences that are directly opposed to their own on all dimensions, when in fact this isn't true.[42] In the instance of the Orange Sisters, it would be akin to the first sister swearing that her sibling also wanted the juice when what the second sister truly wanted was the peel.

> Many people falsely believe that the other party has preferences that are directly opposed to their own on all dimensions, when in fact this isn't true.

It's often possible to reach a mediocre negotiation agreement. However, with careful planning and effort, negotiators can optimize their negotiation experience, which will improve their own outcomes as well as the outcomes of their customers, clients, and colleagues.

TRUTH

46

Are you an enlightened negotiator?

Imagine that you're negotiating with your identical twin, a person with a similar personality to yours. How would the negotiation turn out? Lovefest? Catfight? Standoff? If the answer is anything except a win–win lovefest, we've got a problem, Houston. One of you needs to change.

Suppose you're negotiating with a counterparty whom you trust and admire and with whom you wish to have a long-term relationship. How big do you want the pie to be? This is not a trick question. How do you want to slice that large pie? This is a trickier question. You might say, "Down the middle." Or, "Fairly."

Okay, let's change the question. Suppose you're about to negotiate with someone you don't trust, don't like, or don't respect. How big do you want the total pie to be? If you said, "As big as possible," you're right. Now, how do you want to slice this pie? Most people admit that they want to drive the counterparty down to her barely acceptable set of terms to keep all the added value for themselves.

These two extreme cases reveal an important point: Whether we love or hate the other party, trust or distrust her, will see her again or not, we always want to extract the maximum potential value out of a deal. But we may have different reasons for wanting this. In the case where I adore you, I want to divide a large pie between us because I value my own welfare and yours. In the second case, the only reason I want a big pie of resources to divide is that I want to grab every dime for myself, and I know that there will be more for me if I can discover it.

> Whether we love or hate the other party, trust or distrust her, will see her again or not, we always want to extract the maximum potential value out of a deal.

Thus, one of the key revelations related to win–win negotiations is that we should always want to maximize the pie, regardless of circumstance or whether we are altruists or opportunists. Win–win negotiation can be used solely for self-interest, but it is also the best strategy in completely altruistic negotiations.

It would be naïve to believe that the counterparties you encounter in life are not just as smart and motivated as you are. The enlightened negotiator embraces the fact that the counterparty is smart, ambitious, and has complex, multifaceted motivations.

One of my earliest experiences with enlightened negotiations came at a large pharmaceutical company engaged in a multiday negotiation training program. "We've invited key clients to this training," the pharmaceutical folks who had

> Win–win negotiation can be used solely for self-interest, but it is also the best strategy in completely altruistic negotiations.

developed the program told me. I was aghast—they had invited the "enemy" to hear all their negotiation secrets! They went on to explain that they strongly preferred that the people with whom they negotiate daily be just as expert as they were in the skill of deriving mutual gains through win–win agreements. This was a revelation for me. One of the worst fates that can befall you as a negotiator is to have to reach an agreement with someone who knows a lot less about negotiation than you do. The unenlightened negotiator often hasn't unbundled the negotiation or prioritized—or even considered—his interests; thus, he clings to positions and demands as if they were rafts in a stormy ocean.

The enlightened negotiator, on the other hand, realizes that the best counterparty would in fact be her identical twin—someone who is every bit as knowledgeable, smart, and motivated as she is.

References

Truth 5

1   Thompson, L. L., and Hastie, R. (1990). "Social perception in negotiation." *Organizational Behavior and Human Decision Processes*, 47, 98–123, and Thompson, L. L., and Hrebec, D. (1996). "Lose–lose agreements in interdependent decision making." *Psychological Bulletin*, 120, 396–409.

2   Tinsley, C. H., O'Connor, K. M., and Sullivan, B. A. (2002). "Tough guys finish last: The perils of a distributive reputation." *Organizational Behavior and Human Decision Processes*, 88, 621–642.

Truth 6

3   Osborn, A. F. (1963). *Applied Imagination* (3rd ed.). New York: Scribner.

Truth 7

4   Fisher, R., and William Ury, W. (1983). *Getting to Yes: Negotiating Agreement Without Giving In*. New York: Penguin Books.

Truth 13

5   Galinsky, A. D., and Mussweiler, T. (2001). "First offers as anchors: The role of perspective-taking and negotiator focus." *Journal of Personality and Social Psychology*, 81, 657–669.

Truth 15

6   Galinsky, A. D., and Mussweiler, T. (2001). "First offers as anchors: The role of perspective-taking and negotiator focus." *Journal of Personality and Social Psychology*, 81, 657–669.

Truth 19

7   Frustrated by the low incidence of question asking and information sharing by negotiators, I took a drastic measure: I coached them to reveal information. In one investigation, I told negotiators in no uncertain terms to provide information to the other party. In the study, I compared three groups of people: revealers, questioners, and a control group. I told the revealers to share their interests with the other party and the questioners to ask about the counterparty's interests. The control group received no specific instructions. The results were dramatic:

The revealers and the questioners did much better than the control group in terms of win–win deals. Thus, the revealers and the questioners advanced toward the Pareto Optimal Frontier, while the control group satisficed. So, whether you ask or provide information in a negotiation is less important than just getting it out in the open. Moreover, the effects tended to multiply over time, meaning that as revealers and questioners completed more and more negotiations, they improved their outcomes at a faster rate than the control group. Keep in mind that nothing was preventing the control group from revealing their interests or asking questions. We just relied on their natural reluctance. We did one more critical experiment before telling the world of negotiators that it's not only okay to reveal information but that it's also one of the smartest things to do. Specifically, we had to show that revealing information wouldn't increase the risk of exploitation. So we set up a study in which one negotiator was told to reveal information to the opponent, but the opponent was to avoid revealing any information. This created an asymmetrical situation in which one party knew the interests of the other party but not vice versa. Afterward, we looked for all possible evidence of exploitation—namely poorer performance by the lesser-informed negotiator. We found no evidence of exploitation. In fact, these asymmetrical pairs were much better at expanding the pie and reaching win–win deals on average than the control groups.

8 Thompson, L. (1991). "Information exchange in negotiation." *Journal of Experimental Social Psychology*, 27, 61-179.

Truth 27

9 Tajfel, H. (1970). "Experiments in intergroup discrimination." *Scientific American*, 223, 96–102.

10 Suedfeld, P., Bochner, S., and Matas, C. (1971). "Petitioners attire and petition signing by peace demonstrators: A field experiment." *Journal of Applied Social Psychology*, 1(3), 278–283.

Truth 28

11 Tversky, A., and Kahneman, D. (1974). "Judgment under uncertainty: Heuristics and biases." *Science*, 185, 1124–1131.

12 The 53 UN member states of the African Institute are the following: Algeria, Angola, Benin, Botswana, Burkina Faso, Burundi, Cameroon, Cape Verde, Central African Republic, Chad, Comoros, Congo, Côte d'Ivoire, Democratic Republic of Congo, Djibouti, Egypt, Equatorial Guinea, Eritrea, Ethiopia, Gabon, Gambia, Ghana, Guinea Bissau, Guinea, Kenya, Lesotho, Liberia, Libyan Arab Jamahiriya, Madagascar, Malawi, Mali, Mauritania, Mauritius, Morocco, Mozambique, Namibia, Niger, Nigeria, Rwanda, Sao Tome e Principe, Senegal, Seychelles, Sierra Leone, Somalia, South Africa, Sudan, Swaziland, Tanzania, Togo, Tunisia, Uganda, and Zimbabwe.

Truth 29

13 Tversky, A., and Kahneman, D. (1981). "The framing of decisions and the psychology of choice." *Science*, 211, 45–58.

14 Bazerman, M. H. Magliozzi, T., and Neale, M. A. (1985). "Integrative bargaining in a competitive market." *Organizational Behavior and Human Decision Processes*, 35(3), 294–313.

Truth 30

15 The study was made by my colleagues Ashleigh Rosette of Duke University and Shirley Kopelman of University of Michigan. Kopelman, S., Rosette, A. S., and Thompson, L. (2006). "The three faces of eve: Strategic displays of positive, negative, and neutral emotions in negotiations." *Organizational Behavior and Human Decision Processes*, 99, 81–101.

16 O'Quin, K., and Aronoff, J. (1981). "Humor as a technique of social influence." *Social Psychology Quarterly*, 44, 349–357.

Truth 32

17 Rusbult, C.E., Zembrodt, I.M., and Gunn, L.K.. (1982). "Exit, voice, loyalty, and neglect: Responses to dissatisfaction in romantic involvements." *Journal of Personality and Social Psychology*, 43, 1230-1242.

Truth 33

18 Damast, A. (2012). "She works hard for less money." *Bloomberg Businessweek*, 4310, 31-32.

19 Marks, M., and Harold, C. (2011). "Who asks and who receives in salary negotiation." *Journal of Organizational Behavior*, 32(3), 371–394.

20 Bowles, H. R., Babcock, L., and Lai, L. (2007). "Social incentives for gender differences in the propensity to initiate negotiations: Sometimes it does hurt to ask." *Organizational Behavior and Human Decision Processes*, 103(1), 84–103.

21 Kray, L. J., Thompson, L., & Galinsky, A. (2001). "Battle of the sexes: Gender stereotype confirmation and reactance in negotiations." *Journal of Personality and Social Psychology*, 80, 942-958.

Truth 34

22 Croson, R., and Steven G. (2001). "Reputations in negotiation." In Hoch, S. J., Kunreuther, H. C., and Gunther, R. E. (eds.), *Wharton on Making Decisions* (pp. 177–186). Hoboken, NJ: John Wiley and Sons.

Truth 35

23 Pennebaker, J. W., and Sanders, D. Y. (1976). "American graffiti: Effects of authority and reactance arousal." *Personality and Social Psychology Bulletin*, 2, 264–267.

Truth 37

24 Morton Deutsch, M. (1973). *The Resolution of Conflict: Constructive and Destructive Processes*. Binghamton, NY: Vail-Ballou

25 White, J. B., Tynan, R., Galinsky, A. D., and Thompson, L. (2004). "Face threat sensitivity in negotiation: Roadblock to agreement and joint gain." *Organizational Behavior and Human Decision Processes*, 94, 102–124.

26 Ury, W., Brett, J. M., and Goldberg, S. B. (1993). *Getting Disputes Resolved*. San Francisco: Jossey-Bass.

Truth 38

27 Valley, K. L., Moag, J., and Bazerman, M. H. (1998). "A matter of trust: Effects of communication on the efficiency and distribution of outcomes." *Journal of Economic Behavior and Organizations*, 34, 211–238.

28 Drolet, A. L., and Morris, M. W. (2000). "Rapport in conflict resolution: Accounting for how non-verbal exchange fosters cooperation on mutually beneficial settlements to mixed-motive conflicts." *Journal of Experimental Social Psychology*, 36, 26–50.

Truth 39

29 Smiley, D. (2013, January 5). "The perils of buying a foreclosed home online." *Miami Herald*.

30 McGuire, T. W., Kiesler, S., and Siegel, J. (1987). "Group and computer-mediated discussion effects in risk decision making." *Journal of Personality and Social Psychology*, 52(5), 917–930.

31 Ibid

32 Przybylski, A. & Weinstein, N. (2013). "Can you connect with me now? How the presence of mobile communication technology influences face-to-face conversation quality." *Journal of Social and Personal Relationships*, 30(3) 237-246.

33 Diermeier, D., Huffaker, D., and Swaab, R. I. (2011). "The language of coalition formation in online multiparty negotiations." *Journal of Language and Social Psychology*, 30(1), 66–81.

34 Swaab, R. I., Maddux, W., and Sinaceur, M. (2011). "Virtual linguistic mimicry: When and how online mimicry increases negotiation outcomes." *Journal of Experimental Social Psychology*, 47, 616–621.

Truth 40

35 Boone, A. L., and Mulherin, J. H. (2007). "How are firms sold?" The Journal of Finance, 62, 847–875.

Truth 42

36 Tharp, Bruce (2009). "Four organizational culture types." White paper, Haworth Organizational Culture. Haworth.com

Truth 43

37 Morris, M. W., & Peng, K. (1994). "Culture and cause: American and Chinese attributions for social and physical events." *Journal of Personality and Social Psychology*. 67(6), 949-971.

Truth 44

38 Ury, W., Brett, J. M., and Goldberg, S. B. (1993). *Getting Disputes Resolved*. San Francisco: Jossey-Bass.

Truth 45

39 Tverksy, A., and Kahneman, D. (1974). "Judgment under uncertainty: Heuristics and biases." *Science*, 185, 1124-1131.

40 Fry, W. R., Firestone I., and Williams, D. L. (1983). "Negotiation process and outcome of stranger dyads and dating couples: Do lovers lose?" *Basic and Applied Psychology*, 4(1), 1.

41 In 1983, Max Bazerman and Margaret Neale coined the term fixed-pie perception to refer to this spurious belief. Bazerman, M., and Neale, M. (1983). "Heuristics in negotiation: Limitations to effective dispute resolution." *Research in Organizational Behavior*, 9, 247–288.

42 I began to ponder how entrenched the fixed-pie perception is. For example, I wondered whether people in perfect agreement in reality would still see themselves in complete conflict. If one sister wanted oranges and the other wanted apples, would they still falsely assume that they were in competition? To investigate this, I created a scenario in which people negotiated face to face over eight issues. Two of the eight issues were ones in which negotiators had perfectly compatible interests, which should have resulted in full, mutually beneficial agreement on those issues. Depressingly, 25 percent of negotiators suboptimized on those issues, settling for something worse than what both of them wanted, making needless sacrifices. And among those who actually optimized on that issue, more than 50 percent did not know that they had optimized (that the other party had interests perfectly compatible with theirs). This was major empirical evidence of the pervasiveness of win–lose thinking.

Acknowledgments

In negotiation, there is always a "hidden table," or a group of people who are the real decision makers that might not be visible. This book is no exception. This book is lovingly dedicated to all the students who've suffered through my MBA and executive classes throughout the 20 years that I've been teaching. Their questions, provocations, and stories are echoed in this book. Larissa Tripp at the Kellogg Teams and Groups Center pulled together the drafts and made order out of chaos. Russ Hall did fantastic editing of my feeble drafts. My colleagues and collaborators, Max Bazerman, Jeanne Brett, Adam Galinsky, Shirli Kopelman, Laura Kray, Jeff Loewenstein, Kathleen McGinn, Don Moore, Michael Morris, Janice Nadler, Ashleigh Rosette, Elizabeth Seeley, and Judith White provided the intellect and enthusiasm to build a community of negotiation research that inspired this book. My family, Anna, Ray, Sam, and Bob, gives me the encouragement to keep on plugging when I did not feel like plugging any more.

About the Author

Leigh Thompson is a Distinguished Professor of Dispute Resolution & Organizations at the Kellogg School of Management at Northwestern University. She directs the Leading High Impact Teams executive program, the Kellogg Team and Group Research Center, and co-directs the Negotiation Strategies for Managers program. An active scholar and researcher, she has published more than 110 research articles and chapters and has authored 9 books, including: *Creative Conspiracy: The New Rules of Breakthrough Collaboration, The Mind and Heart of the Negotiator, Making the Team, Organizational Behavior Today, Creativity and Innovation in Organizational Teams, Shared Knowledge in Organizations, Negotiation: Theory and Research, The Social Psychology of Organizational Behavior,* and *Conflict in Organizational Groups.* Thompson speaks and conducts workshops on negotiation teamwork, collaboration, and creativity skills for large and small organizations across the globe.

Visit her at: www.LeighThompson.com.